Antiques *for* Today's Interiors

Antiques *for* Today's Interiors

GENEVIEVE WEAVER AND HELEN CHISLETT

Guinevere Antiques

COLLINS & BROWN

First published in Great Britain in 1999
by Collins & Brown Limited
London House
Great Eastern Wharf
Parkgate Road
London SW11 4NQ

Distributed in the United States and Canada by
Sterling Publishing Co, 387 Park Avenue South,
New York, NY 10016, USA

1 3 5 7 9 8 6 4 2

British Library Cataloguing-in-Publication Data:
A catalogue record for this book
is available from the British Library.

ISBN 1 85585 7065 (hardback edition)

Editor: Mary Lambert
Designer: David Fordham
Photography: Andreas von Einsiedel

Reproduction by Classic Scan Pte Ltd, Singapore
Printed and bound in Hong Kong

Contents

Foreword

THE FIRST ANTIQUE I EVER BOUGHT WAS IN London – a walnut Spanish table for which I paid £100 in 1959. At the time, I was living in a futuristic house in Notting Hill that I had designed myself. The staircase resembled a huge steel ladder going from the bottom of the house right to the top – the steps were attached to this, giving the whole effect a visual twist. Everything was steel, wood, slate, glass brick and, with the exception of that table, brand new. My favourite shops at the time were Heal's, Liberty and Woolland. My taste was for the perfect simplicity of modern Scandinavian furniture. A motley collection of stools and chairs was arranged around my walnut table, but even then I liked the effect of old and new.

I have a very low boredom threshold where possessions are concerned. It was this that first ignited my passion for antiques. My house in Portobello Road was amazing for its day, but I began to tire of it. After two years, I wanted to change my furniture completely. It was then I realized the true advantage of antique furniture over modern: you can lose money on antiques, but you won't lose everything. They always retain some sort of resale value. But the same could not be said for modern furniture – most of it was thrown away. So I began to look at antiques differently. Not only did they offer an economic advantage over modern furniture, but the resale aspect meant that – in theory – I could buy whatever I wanted, enjoy living with it for a while, then sell it on. What could be more perfect for a person who always longed for a change?

From the very beginning, I never looked at antiques from a conventional point of view. I was not particularly interested in the significance of a piece; what actually counted for me was its form, shape, colour and texture – in other words, the visual statement it was going to make within a room. It seemed obvious to me that you didn't need many things to make an impact – what you needed was one wonderful piece from which you could build up an entire scheme.

Antiques often combined materials that were visually stunning: tortoiseshell and silver perhaps, or lacquer and straw-work, but were no longer widely available. This added to their aesthetic excitement as well as their rarity. Because everything was hand-crafted, the attention to detailing was superb. And nothing was exactly like something else – the infinite variety within pieces was fascinating. I began by looking at them with an artist's eye and then became more and more involved and fascinated as my knowledge grew.

Now I still allow myself to be led by my eye and my heart, not by budget. If you see something you absolutely love, then you should buy it – for the simple reason you might never find it again. Don't worry about investing money wisely: the antiques market, like any other, can make you money or lose you money. What matters is how high your heart leaps when you first set eyes on a piece, and whether you can immediately see it in the context of your home. It is that heady rush of adrenaline that still keeps me in the business I love today.

GENEVIEVE WEAVER

Chapter 1 In *the* beginning

LEFT Genevieve Weaver in her indigo-and-woad dining room. On the wall is a collection of drainers, mainly 18th and 19th century, which she has been collecting for over 35 years and has arranged with a practised eye. They are among the few things that she would hate to be parted from.

ARRIVED IN LONDON from Normandy in 1953 at the age of 22. At the time, I was a hat designer and I found a job working for an old-fashioned manufacturer called McCracken & Bowen. I only meant to stay one year, but I had such fun that I arranged to take English lessons, and before long my teacher had become my mother-in-law.

My husband bought a plot of land in the Portobello Road for £900 and we built the space-age house I described earlier. I had my first son, Kevin, in 1959 – the same year as I bought that Spanish walnut table. Fittingly, he is now a director of Guinevere. Then we moved to Switzerland briefly where my second son, Marc, was born – he too has become a director of the company.

When we returned to London in 1963, we moved to Chelsea. The shops at the 'wrong' end of the King's Road were then virtually going for nothing. It

9

was here that you would have found the gas works and the council estate, the fish-and-chip shop and the laundry, the betting shop, the workmen's café and the local butcher. It was hardly the place from which to launch an internationally acclaimed antiques emporium, but all I wanted was a humble shop. My rent for No. 578 was £7 per week. Now rents and prices have escalated so far that none of the original life and commerce of the street has survived. This part of the King's Road is now an antiques ghetto, with only pubs and restaurants to break up the richly filled shop fronts.

SELLING ANTIQUES

I was bored with hat design by this time, and thought I could have a go at selling antiques. At that time, they were very cheap to buy. To begin with I had a partner, a man called Tom Jones; he said he would buy the goods for me to sell in the shop because I knew absolutely nothing at all. We worked together for about a year. The problem was that his taste and philosophy were not mine – he bought pieces just to make a profit. I wanted only what I had a feeling for – I have never liked ugly pieces of Victoriana, for example. In my view if

LEFT A view of this section
of the Kings Road as it
looked in 1963. At that
stage, Guinevere was
already so full of stock that
much of it spilt out into the
street. Today the shop has
expanded into sites at
either side and boasts one
of the largest shop fronts.

something was ugly in the nineteenth century, it will still be ugly in the twenty-first. There is no point in selling pieces that you don't like yourself.

So after a year I decided to go it alone. I started by selling pine furniture because it was so cheap. I could buy a chest-of-drawers for £1 or £2, clean, strip and wax it, add brass handles, then sell it on for £6 to £12. I was drawn towards pine because it had the same clean, simple feel to it as the Scandinavian furniture I had once liked so much. Word spread around the other dealers, and soon I had built up a healthy business selling pine on in the trade.

THE GUINEVERE STYLE

Then came my big break. My landlord made me close the shop for eight months while the building was being renovated. At the same time, I was given the chance to buy the entire contents of a London workhouse, which I did for £140. I had to rent a warehouse for a year as there was so much stock. I had about 30 farmhouse tables, five huge kitchen dressers, numerous kitchen chairs, chests-of-drawers and all sorts of other things. Each week, I would clean and wax another table and take it round to all the antique shops I knew until I found a buyer. In this way, I built up enough capital to invest in other furniture for the business. When I reopened, I set the style for the shop that people see today – the

window looked fantastic. I papered the walls in wrapping paper, laid vinyl upside down so that I had a white floor, placed a piece of beautifully waxed pine furniture centre stage, and then just finished off the whole look with a bowl of perfect lemons. It looked stunning. Guinevere was launched.

By now, I had a new business partner – John Arnett. He began by helping me strip furniture, but we had the same eye for pieces and enthusiasm for antiques, and before long he was accompanying me on buying trips around the country. I divorced my husband in 1975, and John and I became partners in every sense of the word.

Our first buying trips were mad affairs. We would take a van to Lancashire, Yorkshire, Derbyshire. Cheshire, Northamptonshire, Wales or the west country, and fill it up with furniture within a day.

SEARCHING FOR STOCK

The whole of Britain was a gold mine then. We would buy chests, cupboards, dressers, chairs, clocks, paintings, mirrors – anything that we thought we could trade on fast. After stripped pine, we moved into English oak furniture because it was so neglected. We would buy the most fabulous huge Jacobean dressers or beds, then sell them on to the French dealers we knew. The English were not interested in buying that period at all – they

11

RIGHT The basement of Guinevere, with vaulted ceilings, where coal was once stored. It is no wonder that so many customers describe the shop as an Aladdin's cave or – if they are French – la cave d'Ali Baba. It is big, and at any one time is likely to hold about 3,000 items of stock.

only wanted conventional Georgian mahogany furniture.

But word began to spread, and soon American, German and Dutch customers were elbowing each other out of the way to see what we had in stock. We only sold to the trade: that way we could move goods on at a fast enough rate to make a decent profit. I kept an eye on what they were buying and bought stock to fit the demand. However, I also made sure that I bought pieces I liked well enough to put in the shop window. But I have to say that it was always buying, rather than selling, that gave me the biggest thrill.

That is not to say we didn't allow private customers into the shop. People at the cutting edge of fashion and design were starting to see the decorative potential in antiques. I was not interested in selling antiques for their value – I liked them because of the visual impact they could have in a room, and the excitement of being able to mix old with new. This approach was absolutely in tune with the sixties, 'anything goes' attitude. So it was not unusual to find Mick Jagger browsing around the shop or Jean Shrimpton dropping by to see what was new. Derek Nimmo, John le Mesurier, Lauren Bacall, Hayley Mills, Laurence Harvey and many others also became regular and appreciative visitors to the shop. Some of the glamour that they brought with them began to rub off on us, and the name Guinevere became synonymous not so much with antiques as with antiques with attitude.

When I look back on those days, I feel nostalgic

Right The ground floor of
Guinevere where a pair of fine
cast iron torchères of
American Indians stand sentry.
They were made in the Val
d'Osne factory in 1890 by
Salmson and are very rare.
The Weavers are in no hurry
to part with such models.

not just for the sheer quantity of antiques available
and their prices, but also for the characters that we
knew. There was Johnny Whiskers down the
Portobello Road, for example, a lovable rogue if ever
there was one, and also Mr Grosvenor who lived in
Leek, whose stock seemed to be wholly supplied by
Irish tinkers.

A CAST OF CHARACTERS

As a young French woman, I met dealers – usually
men – who would patronize me. But others treated
me with enormous kindness and gave me a great
deal of help and advice. So at times being a woman,
particularly one with a French accent, was an asset,
not a hindrance. There was Alan Henry in Bolton
who first introduced me to pine Dutch cupboards
and other wonderful items. If there was something I
liked but could not afford, he would tell me to take
it and pay for it when I had the money. Joe Marshall
in Blackburn was equally generous – if I could not
afford something from his amazing stock, he would
tell me to take it and return it if it did not sell. It
always did. In return, I made sure that we always
paid when we said we would and that our cheques
never bounced. As the years went on, people began
to realize that they could trust the Guinevere name.

They were good days, but we did work hard. I
remember leaving at four one morning, and not

returning until seven the following morning, having
had no sleep. Then there was the time we drove
through a snow-storm and I had to keep my hands
on the windscreen to act as a primitive de-icer. On
that same trip, we had arranged to go back to a shop
later and pick up some furniture. We arrived late at
night to find that the dealer had left the goods for us
on the pavement outside his shop, but we had no
rope with which to tie it onto the van. So I had to
climb over fences into people's gardens and
surreptitiously steal their washing lines.

13

RIGHT One of Guinevere's strengths is that, wherever possible, the Weavers try to display antiques in room settings – such as this intimate dining scene. The chairs are Louis XV carved giltwood, covered in a wonderful Aubusson tapestry.

I have to confess that we were also the vandals of our day – we simply didn't know any better to begin with. There was such an abundance of items that we acted with irreverence towards them. I shudder to think of the pine pieces I stripped that were probably Georgian, or the patinas we destroyed in our bid to improve certain pieces of furniture. Perhaps worst of all were the long-case clocks we bastardized into broom cupboards by removing the workings and polishing the cases. Believe it or not, that was one of the only ways of persuading people to buy clocks they regarded as junk.

THE LEARNING CURVE

We picked up knowledge as we went. Every weekend for two years I would go to the Victoria & Albert Museum and study particular pieces of furniture. But it was so frustrating not to be able to examine them closely, turn them upside down or feel them. In the end, I decided it was a pointless way of trying to educate myself.

Most of what I learnt came from other people in the trade. I relied on my instinct and my eyes, but sometimes I was able to apply the little knowledge that I had and that gave me great satisfaction. For example, on one occasion when I was told about a nineteenth–century barley twist, gate-leg table, my immediate reaction was to turn it down, sight unseen.

But when I did see it, I realized it was in fact seventeenth-century but had been stripped and polished so much it looked Victorian – so I bought it. I remember the expert on early oak furniture coming to take a look at it to see whether I was right. He had shoulder-length red hair, a big beard and dandyish clothes. I can still see him lying on the floor under the table with his hair spread out on the floor saying, 'You are absolutely right. This is seventeenth-century.' It is moments like that which have given me the greatest kick.

LOOKING FURTHER AFIELD

As the years went by and the antiques trade in this country boomed, we began to look further afield for our merchandise. To begin with, that meant buying trips to France, Holland or other European countries. But about 20 years ago I began to realize the potential in places further afield, such as India, China, Vietnam, Pakistan, Thailand, Singapore and other exotic locations.

Now I have stepped back from the day-to-day running of Guinevere. Kevin and Marc run the business and financial side, while Marc's wife Heather runs the shop floor. Over the years I have built up a wonderful team, including my right-hand man Rob Hunter, whose eye for detail ensures the shop always looks fabulous. Then there are the

specialist restorers who work from our own work-shop. Many of them, such as Michael Folkard who is responsible for the specialist paint effects, have been with Guinevere for a great many years. I am now in the happy position of being able to concentrate on those aspects of the business which have always given me the greatest pleasure – buying antiques from all around the world, overseeing the look and feel of the shop, and of course working with Rob to design those famous shop-front windows.

The premises have naturally had to expand to cope with the increasing scale of the business. The original shop has expanded into neighbouring sites and is now the size of four shops. I bought the freehold a long time ago, so there is no landlord to pay my £7 per week rent to now. It is all such a far cry from the days of laboriously stripping pine chests to make a £5 profit, or stealing washing lines to use as rope.

GENEVIEVE WEAVER   15

Chapter 2 The *Philosophy*

OPPOSITE This sumptuous bedroom scene, with the *lit à la Polonaise* at its centre, is another example of a Guinevere room set. It is draped in 20 antique Paisleys.

LEFT Piles of vellum-bound (pigskin) books are piled up the stairs of the shop. Vellum was commonly used before leather and most of these are written in Latin.

GUINEVERE'S PARTICULAR PHILOSOPHY OF GOOD trading, aesthetic sensitivity and a strong awareness of current design carries lessons for anyone incorporating antiques into a contemporary setting. The pieces they choose are objects to live with rather than revere. Having the Dead Sea Scrolls would be of no interest here. The message at the heart of the Guinevere philosophy is that antiques and antiquities are not just rare and ancient objects to be displayed within a museum-style setting. They can be used to give that decorative focal point to a room. That means choosing colours and shapes that complement them, and building up a room scheme around them.

The second point to note is that antiques are not removed from fashion, but very often reflect precisely what is happening stylistically. It is important to keep your fingers firmly on the pulse of

RIGHT One thing that Genevieve Weaver stresses to customers is the importance of finding a centrepiece for a room. In her own drawing room, a handsome bed by Jean-Jacques Werner with ormolu detailing takes pride of place. The French bishop's chair is carved giltwood, and is *circa* 1750.

OPPOSITE This Venetian 18th century mirror with silver leaf another example of the sort of anchor piece in which Guinevere specializes. It is handsome enough not to nee props. But here a biscuit-glaz pierrot, one of Genevieve's own extensive collection, provides a charming touch.

design. The Weavers are not concerned with helping people create a pastiche of the past, so much as looking at ways of showing how relevant antiques are to contemporary interiors. Professional designers and decorators, of which many have cooperated with this book, visit the shop because they know they will find unusual, eye-catching and dominating pieces as opposed to conventional pieces of brown wood furniture.

From the very beginning, the shop has been at the cutting edge of what is happening in the design world, and has started, revived and echoed many trends that have had a huge impact on interior design. Genevieve and her team were stripping pine furniture back in the early sixties – years before it ever became fashionable. Over the past four decades other interior fashions they have introduced include: English oak furniture, metal French café chairs, painted French armoires, old tapestry cushions, chicken-wire cupboard doors, tea-stained fabrics, Anglo-Indian furniture, oriental red lacquer, calligraphy on walls, black-and-gold picture frames and 2,000 year-old antiquities including stick men from the tombs of China. Many of these have now become ubiquitous on the pages of design magazines, but could have been found on the shop floor years before becoming universally popular.

HOW TO BUY THE GUINEVERE WAY

When buying antiques from a decorative point of view, you must be disciplined: assess the look, style, originality and age. But if there is no visual impact, don't take it any further. If something looks fabulous enough to buy, then assess it in terms of quality and how that quality is reflected in the price. If the quality isn't there, you have to decide whether style alone is enough to make it worth buying.

LEFT Always use a lot of something rather than a little if you want to make a visual statement. These orange tree enamelled cast-iron planters, made by E. Paris et Cie in 1860, are carefully arranged to reflect the curve of the stairs. The sheer number of them gives aesthetic impact.

RIGHT This collection of blue-and-white Chinese porcelain dates mainly from the 18th and 19th centuries. It looks as though it is part of a haul from a salvaged cargo ship but, in fact, is part of the stock on the shop floor. The painted and giltwood table is an Italian design.

no-one will buy it. So, what you would not find on the shop floor, in simple terms, is the ordinary, the ugly or the uninteresting. If a chair was made with legs too squat in the eighteenth century, time will not have improved its proportions at all. It was ugly then and it will still be ugly today.

What you will find in the shop – as well as in this inspiring book – are dozens of pieces, from large to small, that have been hand-picked for their aesthetic charms and their excellent quality. You should also find ideas on how to use them in your own home when decorating. It is a question of training the eye to recognize how strong they can be in a room setting.

FINDING A FOCUS

It is focal points or anchor pieces which give a room its strength. These are the design statements within a room – it could be a piece of furniture, a chandelier, a mirror, a painting, or a collection of some sort. It is often overscaled. Size really does matter when you are aiming for something that looks amazing to be the centre of your scheme. Even in a small room, one big piece is going to make all the difference. Because of this, you should always

The difference between Guinevere and many other antiques shops is that you will find objects that are visually satisfying rather than those that might be important because they are the best of their particular period. In fact, a piece of exceptional quality might not make the grade because it does not please the eye as much as it should. However, there is also a very practical down-to-earth approach in evidence: the pieces sold must be functional as well as beautiful. If the drawers of a chest-of-drawers are not deep enough, for example,

RIGHT There is always a demand for instant collections among decorators and those who want to bring immediate interest into a home. Gilt ormolu frames, *circa* 1900, are just one of the items that Guinevere specializes in. The inkwell in the foreground is Napoleon III, *circa* 1870.

try to favour the handsome over the pretty, the unusual over the ubiquitous.

You then have to use your imagination when it comes to the potential which that piece offers. A sleek Chinese table does not mean you must opt for a chinoiserie room, just as a Regency armchair does not mean you must be confined to that one period. Think laterally and look beyond the history of the object. Consider the lines it forms, its texture and its patina, its colour and its size. Think of the effect it will have when juxtaposed with pieces from other countries of origin and different centuries.

The key thing to remember is that a decorative context for antiques does not necessarily mean a traditional one. The eclectic approach – the idea of mixing styles together – has been a core part of decorators' schemes for many years now. This means that antique objects are as relevant to modern interiors as they are to period ones. What matters is the unique combination of decorative ingredients that dominate no matter how old something is. There are no rules other than what pleases the eye. For example, you could combine that nineteenth-century Chinese table with an Art Deco mirror very successfully; or team an extravagant ivory-and-silver bedhead from nineteenth–century India with a grey-flannel-upholstered Regency chair.

Perhaps you would like to introduce a baroque giltwood throne into an otherwise minimalist interior; or place a 1,000-year–old pot in the gleaming modernity of a chic city bathroom. Visual impact and the excitement of the unexpected are what today's interiors are all about.

Remember too that your centrepiece should be dressed to the nines to give it even more impact. Dressers, bookcases, beds and tables are all

RIGHT A rather unusual collection of glass ball clocks from the late 19th century is arranged on leather-bound books in this collector's library. There are English, Swiss and American designs here, their surrounds made particularly attractive with coloured paste stones.

examples of furniture that take on a new level of beauty when properly dressed. When deciding on your budget, try to allow for the extras you will need to show your chosen piece off to its full potential.

THE IMPORTANCE OF DISPLAY

It cannot be over-emphasized how much of a difference you can make within a room if you think about how possessions are displayed. People often spend a lot of money on furniture, paintings and other objects, but spend very little time styling them.

It is true that some people have more of an eye for arranging a room than others, but with so many books and magazines to provide inspiration, it is possible to learn a lot just by looking closely at what other people do. Instant collections are popular with those who do not have the time or the desire to build one up from scratch. Decoratively, they bring

immediate character and visual strength into any room. But all this can be lost if they are not first grouped together for the maximum aesthetic effect. You must think about where the collection is to be placed; how you are going to house it; whether you want it to be seen from eye level when someone is standing, or whether you would prefer to display it so that it is viewed well from a sitting position.

The same is true if you are buying paintings or other objects to be hung on the walls. Think about how best to group pictures together, how much space to leave between them, how to light them, how to make sure they are seen well by both day and night. It is not enough to write out a cheque and take your prize home – you should carry with you a mental picture of the room where you are planning to put something and then plan carefully how you are going to dress it.

23

OPPOSITE Decorators such as Californian Judy Wilder search through Guinevere looking for attention-grabbing pieces, such as this elaborate Venetian mirror. Displayed in the cabinets is Judy's own collection of rare 18th-century Chinese tobacco leaf porcelain. The huge urn in the background is fine *blanc de chine*, one of a pair.

RIGHT This handsome gilt bronze classical urn is perfectly juxtaposed with a Vienna bronze of a boy riding an ostrich. Made by Bergmann – the best and most prolific maker of cold-painted bronzes – it is a particularly collectible piece because the subject matter is so rare.

THE ECONOMICS OF ANTIQUES

It seems obvious that buying antiques make sense not just aesthetically but economically too. A lot of the items, particularly furniture, would cost the same if you bought them new. Yet the antique version retains a sell-on value, which few modern pieces have. That is not to say that you cannot lose money on them – the antiques market is no different from any other and prices go down as well as up. But you are virtually guaranteed to recoup some of your initial investment, and in most cases you can make money. Having said that you should buy something because you love it, not just with investment in mind. If you are buying in a recession, only buy an item that is going cheap or which is so heart-stoppingly wonderful you cannot ignore it. If you are buying in a buoyant economy, remember that antiques also lose value if a recession follows later.

The big difference in price comes with decorative *objets d'art*, such as tortoiseshell tea caddies or ivory figures. What adds to the expense is that these have far more visual impact when part of a collection. However, it is possible to buy good reproductions of such things, which would cost hundreds of pounds as opposed to thousands for an original. If you are only concerned with the aesthetics then there is an argument to say that buying fakes is acceptable. But it might be that you are drawn towards originals because you appreciate them more deeply. If so, you will never be happy with reproductions. Collecting antiques is a learning curve; the pieces that you buy at one stage in your life are not necessarily the ones you like a few years later. By this stage you will know more, and will want to improve your collection. This is the stage where you begin to cross the boundary between being an enthusiast and a connoisseur.

Decorating *with* Antiques

T HE FIRST THINGS TO TACKLE ARE THE BONES OF a room. Decorating decisions focusing on how to use the space, which colour scheme to opt for, or how best to display much loved objects must still be taken. The difference when using antiques is that these become integral to each choice you make, affecting as they do scale, surface, form and texture.

The joy of decorating around antiques is that they give you a new viewpoint on each stage of putting a scheme together. Rather than deciding, for example, on colours and then looking for furniture which is sympathetic to them, you find yourself thinking in a more lateral way. By finding the core pieces first – those that anchor a room together – you can make other decorating decisions with more confidence. In many ways there is less to think about because the spotlight is fixed so firmly on the shape, style, patina and ornamentation intrinsic to whichever antique you have placed centre stage.

In this section of the book, we break down the design process into recognizable and coherent stages: assessing the space you have; choosing an anchor piece; tackling colour; introducing pattern and texture; displaying collections effectively; and how to achieve a contemporary mixture of period and global styles.

LEFT The architectural bones of this home - doors, cornicing, dados – create a perfect canvas on whcih to introduce key pieces of furniture. Vistas from one room into another have been carefully considered, so unifying the scheme as a whole.

27

Chapter 3 Assessing *Space*

LEFT A rich design of backlit stained glass showing a pastoral scene has been used to powerful effect in this bathroom. Its double height results in a cathedral-like space which distracts from the narrow nature of the room. Mirrored arches set into the walls continue the trick of the eye.

OPPOSITE A hallway should be treated as a room in its own right. If you have a generous space and attractive architectural features you should look for ways of emphasizing the proportions, as the bold geometric design on this floor does. The positioning of the furniture reflects these motifs.

WHEN DESIGNING A ROOM, MOST PEOPLE look at the space they have and buy furniture, accessories and other items to fit. Instead you should try to think in a slightly different way. Study all the rooms that you have. Look at their proportions, views, architectural detailing and period, natural light and so on. Then think about how they are used and who by: consider any other members of the family, pets and friends.

Does the function of a room alter from day to night or winter to summer? Consider whether you need flexibility and if each space fulfils its purpose.

Where possible, look for ways of improving the space you have. The bones of a room are the doors, windows, cornicing, picture rails and skirting boards. You should give these more emphasis by making them as large as possible. They are the frame of the canvas on which you will then work.

immediately in that room. Once you have found the starting point, you can build the scheme around it.

This approach is integral to the idea of decorating with antiques. Because of their individuality, their rarity and their uniqueness, you cannot buy them to fit. You cannot copy a picture seen in a magazine or a book because you will probably never find a piece exactly like the one you so admire. You could commission a reproduction piece, but this doesn't make sense either economically or aesthetically. Reproductions have very little sell-on value in comparison to the genuine article. And they do not have the same integrity as the original does. If you put an eighteenth-century bookcase next to a modern copy, the difference would be glaringly obvious – not so much in shape, size or form but in the materials used and the texture on the surface of the furniture. So you need to accept at the very beginning that you don't buy antiques to fit a space, but that you create a space around antiques.

TRAFFIC AREAS

You must think about how people actually move around the house from room to room, and how to link one area to the next. These so-called traffic areas are the skeleton of your home: the bones that keep everything else together. The hallway is the invitation to the rest of the house. It sets the tone, so

You might also consider altering rooms by extending, knocking through or partitioning off areas. Naturally, you have to weigh the financial outlay against the predicted results, but it could be money well spent if the result is a better proportioned, lighter and larger room.

Once you are happy with the space at your disposal, start thinking about how you can bring out its full potential through furnishings and decoration. Carry around a mental picture of what the room looks like when you search for the right item. It is important to find a starting point – perhaps a piece of furniture, a work of art, an architectural addition – that you can visualize

*Quite often there are problems with the proportions of a room to start with;
a limit to what you can do. I use antique furniture to trick the eye
into imagining the walls and ceilings of a room
have expanded – perhaps by introducing an enormous bookcase,
bed or screen which in effect changes the scale of the room.*

ALIDAD

LEFT Well placed furniture can give the impression of there being more space than really exists. This landing is fairly narrow but the use of a large oil painting in a central position expands the walls. The scale of the console table, chairs and lighting sconces emphasizes the approach.

it is important to make sure that visitors will feel uplifted as they walk in. The most important lesson is to treat the hallway as you would any other room. It is more than just a through-route: it is the first space that is encountered on walking in. This matters not only because it gives guests first impressions, but also because you yourself want to feel a sense of comfort and happiness as you walk through the front door. So you need to create something special in terms of atmosphere.

It is a major traffic area, so you need to think carefully about the routes that are taken through the hall. Safety and practicality count as much as aesthetics – hard floors are wonderful, but don't polish them into something resembling an ice-rink. Make sure too that stairs are well lit and that there are banisters for people to hold on to if they lose their footing.

You also have to think about how the hall links to the other areas within the house. Can you see into another room? If so, the view should be as inviting as possible. Also think about whether it is clear where guests should leave their coats or wet umbrellas, or which direction they should go in.

Look at the staircase as well. If it is beautiful architecturally, think how you are going to emphasize it even more. Consider, too, how you are going to make the link from stairs to hall or stairs to

33

landing. Perhaps there are 'dead' spaces, such as stairwells or awkward corners, which you are not sure how to handle. The trick is to make something of them rather than try to ignore them – find something beautiful to display here, light it well, and you suddenly have a feature rather than a flaw.

The beauty of hallways, stairwells and landings from a decorative point of view is that you can push the boundaries out here. They are the perfect spaces in which to display works of art or one really sumptuous piece of furniture. Even in a small hallway, you should go for maximum visual impact by buying one or two items that are large enough to immediately hold the eye as you enter.

STORAGE CONSIDERATIONS

A home has to function on a practical as well as an aesthetic level, which means assessing not only the space, but what is to go in it. The latter is of course dependent on how you use certain rooms. This is a very personal decision and not one where you necessarily want to follow the conventional path. If you have a passion for collecting, for example, you need to put this high on your list of priorities.

Space is what you pay for when you buy a home, so it makes sense to use every square metre of it well. Good storage is at the heart of this: it is not just about how many cupboards and chests-of-drawers you own, but about making your home work for you on a very individual level. It encompasses both how to maintain possessions well and how to display them effectively. It includes everything from the wine in your cellar and the coats in your hall to space for CDs and hanging pictures with panache.

If you take the example of the main communal space within your home, very often the drawing room, it might well combine a myriad different functions. Perhaps it is the room where you like to

relax and watch television or listen to music; the space in which you entertain friends; a place in which you work; an extra room in which to eat; a children's play area.

However, many people today like to keep such a living area as a quiet space in which to unwind from the stresses of the day or enjoy the companionship of friends. If this idea appeals, look at ways of banishing some of the room's activities and their associated paraphernalia into other areas of the house. On the other hand, you might want to find a way of keeping all the original uses of the room, but look instead at ingenious storage devices for keeping much of it out of your way.

The bedroom is another example of a place that needs excellent storage as a starting point. Begin by thinking about all the activities that go on here. Do you have a separate dressing room or are all your clothes stored here? Consider whether you like to read, work or telephone friends from your bed. You need to think about whether you are happy with those functions; you may feel that you prefer to have a bedroom that is quieter, more sensuous and more indulgent. Dressing rooms are a boon because they allow you to remove so much of the day-to-day chaos of living and enclose it in a dedicated space.

Now apply all this advice to every area of your home. The aim is to end up with one that not only looks sensational, but also runs smoothly.

MAKE THE MOST OF SPACE

Once you have solved functional problems through storage decisions, it is time to consider what sort of atmosphere you hope to create. This is when you have to take note of the architectural features within your home. Assess them both for good and bad points. There are few houses that are so perfect in dimension that improvements could not be made. This does not necessarily mean calling in an architect and a team of builders. Minor faults, maybe a narrow hall, a low ceiling or a badly centred fireplace, can all be improved considerably by clever

RIGHT Even the narrowest of corners can be given importance with the positioning of a decorative focal point. This imposing marble head of Medusa raised on a plinth has the perfect proportions for this niche. It suits the gracious architecture of the hallway ceiling perfectly.

decoration and the use of pieces of furniture or other decorative objects to trick the eye into imagining the room to be better proportioned than it actually is.

It is a question of playing down the bad and highlighting the good. If, for example, you have a particularly beautiful window with a fine view as well, then you need only dress it very simply so focusing the eye on its architectural qualities rather than concealing them in swathes of fabric. If you have elegant mouldings and ceiling roses, consider spending money on the best chandelier you can so that you draw the eye upwards. If you have a fireplace of distinction, make a fuss of it with a mirror, fire irons and anything else that will spotlight its qualities.

But what if you have none of these things? Then it is important to begin shopping around for key pieces, which will in effect make up for the architectural features you are missing. It might be that a table catches your eye or a painting or a carpet – what you need is something so strong in form that it will make an immediate statement to anyone entering the room. From this, you can create the rest of your inspiration.

The idea is to spend money on something that creates visual interest. After all, conversation points are no bad thing when entertaining. Public spaces within your home – the drawing room, dining room and hallway – are therefore perfect spaces in which to introduce a bold painting, a sculpture or a collection of some sort. Such items as these also have the advantage of drawing attention away from any of the spatial faults that the room might have.

In many ways, dining rooms are the most important spaces in which to create ambience conducive to successful entertaining.

Ideally, you want a dining area, whether it is a dedicated dining room or an orangery, that can be used for informal Sunday lunches for family or friends or to host grand dinner parties. The essential thing to remember is that people need to enjoy themselves when eating here. Chairs should be

OPPOSITE Heavily moulded archways and bold architraving emphasize the flow here from one room to the next. Furniture, such as the Russian neoclassical 18th-century table, has been used to punctuate the space. On top of this is an Italian Grand Tour breche marble tazza which provides an impressive decorative focus.

RIGHT Print rooms are a historic way of transforming a narrow space into a gallery. This apartment has been given a Regency feel through the use of toile du jouy fabric which has been cut into ovals and framed. The symmetry of the display complements the bust and other classical references.

comfortable, the lighting soft, the temperature warm and the table generously proportioned. Although the dining table is at the centre of the scheme, it is not necessarily the item you should spend the most money on. Once it is dressed up with linen, cutlery, china, glasses, candles and flowers, no one would know whether it is made of chipboard or cherrywood. Chairs, too, are rarely noticed other than for their comfort, so it is more important to make sure they are well upholstered rather than worrying too much about their provenance. Storage is again paramount: a sideboard provides not just space to store china but also a surface on which to serve food.

LINKING OUTSIDE WITH INSIDE

There is an increasing recognition that gardens, patios and roof terraces are as integral to the home

OPPOSITE This elaborate cast-iron conservatory makes the perfect backdrop for a set of French bistro two-toned wicker furniture from the 1870s, and a Victorian day-bed. The fountain head was original to the house; above this is a mantel on which are displayed pieces from the British Great Exhibition of 1851.

LEFT This Japanese-style pavilion has a wonderful airy feel to it but is cosy enough to be used all through the year thanks to the Scandinavian stove. Painted 19th-century country chairs and late 18th-century coaching tables are a successful addition to an otherwise contemporary room

as a drawing room or kitchen. The fact is that, weather permitting, most people choose to be outside rather than inside. Eating al fresco is particularly joyous – you can almost persuade yourself that the food really does taste better.

Perhaps because of this conventional dining rooms are becoming a rarity these days, so many people now eat instead in kitchens, breakfast rooms or conservatories, many of which link immediately to the garden. These rooms are dual purpose. You can spill out into the garden when the sun is shining or enjoy shelter while still enjoying the view. No wonder then that they have become a key place in which to entertain.

If you do decide to invest in a conservatory, make sure that you light, heat and ventilate it well so that it can be used comfortably all-year round, at any time of day. Always bear in mind how important the vistas are from such rooms; garden lighting is an asset for those who want to dine in style. Happily, there is room for antiques in these rooms too. Now there is a recognition that areas such as this are central to the ambience of a house that they should be treated in exactly the same way as other rooms in terms of design needs. Striking focal points, furniture and beautiful accessories have as much relevance here as they do elsewhere in the home.

Chapter 4 Anchor *pieces*

OPPOSITE This imposing mahogany Empire table, *circa.* 1810, with elaborately carved legs sets the tone in this magnificent library. This outstanding piece would be particularly effective in a hallway or study. A melange of stylized Grand Tour objects emphasizes the classical look.

LEFT A copy of a watercolour, *European Dignitary Being Received By The Great Vazar*, from the Topkapi Palace in Istanbul makes a sensational centrepiece in a theatrical scheme. Its strong colours are echoed in the William IV sofa, which is covered in old Fortuny fabric. The fabric to the left is a 19th-century embroidered European design.

THERE ARE SOME ITEMS THAT YOU FIND, WHICH you know are going to be the centrepiece of a room. You feel as though you could create something really special around them, in fact the sort of room that makes people gasp with admiration when they walk in. Such objects are called anchor pieces. An anchor piece is the dominant item which holds the rest of a decorative scheme together. It may be a piece of furniture, a painting, a carpet, or even a collection of some sort. What matters is the way it holds the eye from the moment you walk into a space.

Anchor pieces are the extroverts of the design world. They demand attention, and you should encourage this. If you have a fabulous dresser, for example, then make a fuss over it. Go out and buy china, glasses or anything else that will do it justice. If it is a magnificent bed, then lavish the best linen

43

and drapes you can afford on it. If it is a painting, always make sure it is well lit both by day and by night. Sometimes you have to add a lot to an acquisition before you really see it at its full potential – at other times, you will find that very little adornment is needed.

Anchor pieces often have a classic quality, a timelessness, which makes them as at home in a modern setting as in a traditional one. They tend to be very strong in shape and form, but not so over-stylized that they would only suit one type of interior. It could be a pair of ebony tables, for example, which look so sleek and simple that you need almost nothing else with them. It might be a statue, an urn, a wall-hanging or something larger, such as a sumptuously upholstered day-bed. You know that you have found the perfect piece when you walk into a shop and, as if by tunnel vision, you

OPPOSITE Maximalists will adore this Victorian Gothic Revival armchair in gilt, with red velvet cushion, because it has a throne-like quality which makes it prominent in any room. Pieces like these can be used in more spartan interiors, in order to create wit and drama in otherwise understated rooms.

LEFT The uncompromising boldness of this Victorian painted coat-of-arms showing lions and fleur-de-lys emphasizes the confidence apparent in this town sitting room. The broken Greek key frieze and the sleekness of the Chinese lacquered cupboard echo the strength of the scheme.

can only see one object in front of you. It is a little like falling in love. The lesson here is that you should always follow your heart.

CHOOSING AN ANCHOR PIECE

Sometimes decorators have specific spaces and measurements in mind and will search for a piece that fits. Try working from the opposite point of view: it is a question of seeing a piece that is so fabulous that you simply have to have it. Then you can create a spectacular scheme around it. At times like this it is essential to buy with the heart and not the head. Buy the thing you love and then create your room around it. You can't expect to create the room first and then find the perfect centrepiece to fit. You will only end up making compromises.

First impressions count. You are buying for yourself and your home, so don't consider something just because you think you might get

used to it or it is in the right price range. You must like it the minute you see it and then assess whether it fits your other criteria.

When you go looking for antiques, you may well want to buy a mirror. But then you might see the most fabulous carpet. You don't really need the carpet, but already you can visualize where it might go and how you would use it to its best advantage. A voice deep down keeps reminding you that what you set out to buy was the mirror, but just ignore that voice. If you feel you really must have the carpet, then buy it. The mirror can be bought another day. Make it a rule in life never to regret anything, and always trust your instincts.

Of course economically, you are buying at a disadvantage. But in the long run, it does not matter. Even if you don't make any money on a piece like this, you will have had the pleasure of owning it for a brief while and feasting your eyes on its aesthetic

47

charms. Antiques are about so much more than monetary value – they are about combining beautiful materials together, craftsmanship, superb detailing and owning a slice of history. Look at them from this point of view and you won't ever regret the ones you buy.

Different types of anchor pieces

Most anchor pieces by definition are big, but it is shape, form, colour and texture that count even more. These are the things that provide the inspiration for the rest of the scheme. Do not buy from an investor's point of view, but from a decorative one. However, having said that the heart must be allowed to rule, it is important to allow the head a say as well. Be practical – size is an important consideration. You must be able physically to get something through the door or up the stairs.

Let us first consider furniture. Look not just at the size and shape of a bed, a bookcase or a table, but at the surface. Imagine an enormous Chinese red leather trunk from the nineteenth century. What catches your eye is the patina on the leather, the enormous double locks and the indigo blue silk lining inside. Versatility is also important. Such a trunk could be used as an ottoman at the foot of a bed, but it could equally take centre stage as a coffee table in a very contemporary living room.

An eighteenth-century black lacquered bookcase also from China might have a surprisingly modern feel to it. Again what makes it so interesting is the way the wood is starting to show through the lacquer. You just can't copy an effect like that, not with all the specialist paint finishes available. It is this textural detail which gives integrity to a piece.

Or perhaps you find a huge French buffet (a china cabinet) from eighteenth-century France, with moulded doors painted in the most sublime combinations of cream, grey and powder blue. Here it might be the slightly distressed finish on the doors that draws the eye, or the depth of the carvings. A piece like this, when dressed with china, looks so stunning you barely need anything else in a room.

Of course an anchor piece doesn't necessarily mean furniture. A handsome pair of architectural paintings could provide all the inspiration you need

As decorators we are trying to create an effect, just as you might on a film set. Antiques contribute tremendously to the atmosphere of an interior because they give a feeling of permanence. The key is finding something at the heart of the scheme which has wonderful texture and form, but also brings a slight frisson of the unexpected. I like to use some whimsical and mad things, rather than just boring brown wood furniture – antiques often introduce some wit to a room.

VIVIEN GREENOCK OF SYBIL COLEFAX AND JOHN FOWLER

to choose colours, fabrics and textures for the room in which they are displayed. Or perhaps it is one enormous gilt mirror, which is so magnificent you would need very little else in a room with it. Collections too can become anchor pieces, but only if they are well displayed so that it is their visual presentation that counts rather than the sheer quantity.

THE EFFECT OF ANCHOR PIECES IN A ROOM

So many people decorate their houses in a rather bland way where nothing dominates. It is as if they are too frightened to go for the one big important piece. Instead, they end up with many small ones dispersed throughout. Yet even in a small room, one big object is going to have treble the impact of 20 small ones.

If you want to create a room which has visual strength, then the rule is: think big. If you can fit it

in, then fit it in. The 'think big' approach is known as overscaling in the trade, and has a long and respectable history in interior design. In fact it is one of the best known tricks from the professional decorator's kit bag.

The point is this: there are very few rooms which are ideal spaces. Perhaps the ceiling is too low, the cornice too small or the proportions are rather mean. You might not have the budget or the inclination to remedy all these things. Instead, you can use a big piece of furniture to counter-balance these architectural faults. For example, in a room with a low ceiling, accentuate height with a very tall screen or a four-poster bed. This tricks the eye into thinking the room is taller than it is.

The mistake is to cram a multitude of fiddly bits and pieces into a small room which then only accentuate the defects of the room. Treating small rooms modestly actually emphasizes their

51

might blow your entire budget on just one thing, but it will be worth it if it makes the room. You can buy everything else you need at some point in the future. The mistake is to stretch out the money you have on lots of objects, where none of them takes on more significance than the others.

DESIGNING FROM AN ANCHOR PIECE

Perhaps the piece that you have bought is so fabulous that you need almost nothing else in the room. But it is much more likely that you will want to build up a scheme from this one central piece. It might be that it provides colour, pattern or texture inspiration. Study it carefully. How are you going to make the most of its shape, its surface, its style? What backdrop could you choose?

When layering up your design scheme, don't forget about lighting. Good lighting can make or break a room's design. Bad lighting can make an interesting room look flat and dull. Anchor pieces deserve to be lit well, because they then take on more significance. This applies not just to paintings, statues and other objects, but also to furniture, where you may want to highlight the surface patina.

problems. The whole point of overscale is that the proportions of the room are no longer obvious – when used properly, it makes a room seem more important and significant. So if you have four walls, don't hang one painting on each of them. Either put the four together or – even better, buy one fabulous floor-to-ceiling portrait or mirror which looks so huge that people immediately think the space must be more generous than it appears. Always go a notch braver than you intended. The idea is that anyone walking in thinks, 'wow'.

Overscaling doesn't only have relevance to small rooms though. If you are lucky enough to have a generously proportioned space, you need to buy objects that will do it justice. If anything, that means going even bigger and more confident again. You

FT Anchor pieces do not
ve to be large of scale;
eresting form or fabulous
namentation are also key
gredients. This elaborate
ian painted-and-gilt urn with
aggerated scrolled handles
a good example as it adds
amusing note to a simple,
odernist interior.

RIGHT A rural Italian landscape in
18th-century style is depicted on this
beautiful silk screen in dusty ochres
and powder greys. Florentine
upholstery fabrics have been chosen
to tone with these muted colours.
Screens are excellent investments
because of their decorative impact
and their manoeuvrability.

Very few people can look at a room and see its final appearance immediately. Most of us need to collect ideas together to help us to make decisions about decorating. You might find it helps to begin by designing a sample board on which a Polaroid of your anchor piece can be pinned. Then around this you can collect everything from paint swatches and fabric samples to photos torn from magazines to decide which direction to take the scheme in.

The beauty of approaching design like this is that you have a physical 3-D object to work from rather than a set of random ideas. You also pick up an idea of how various colours and patterns work together. You can keep playing around with it, adding and removing as you wish, until you think you have the look that you are aiming to achieve.

You might not be able to put it into practice immediately, but the beauty of the anchor piece is that you probably don't need to – it has such strength that it will still look fabulous even when the rest of the room does not. Even if sanding the floorboards and painting the walls is all you can afford, you will have a room with a real sense of style.

The best anchor pieces are those that bring focus to any scheme – be it grand and opulent or sparse and cool. There are some pieces of furniture that are so clean and bold, they could adapt to any interior. Their age and provenance are almost irrelevant – they are prized for their aesthetic qualities and ability to transcend fashions. Many decorators have old favourites from which they would never be parted, no matter how their taste changed.

So allow your eyes and your heart to choose, rather than your cheque book. You are in a no-lose situation anyway, because even if you did make a mistake there will always be someone who loves that piece just as much as you first did. And if you don't buy it now, they may well beat you to it.

Chapter 5 Colour

IF THERE HAS BEEN ONE MAJOR DESIGN REVOLUTION in the last ten years, it has been an explosion of colour. Look through the pages of any glossy homes magazine and you see that this is still the major story of the moment. Yet colour in interior decoration is nothing new; look around any antique shop floor and the intensity of colour will hit you. Now remember that these are shades that have had several hundred years to fade – just think how bright they must have been originally. Colour can be such an uplifting, exciting and stimulating experience. Consider using it in your home to accentuate the positive elements. It is at the core of a decorating scheme, so it makes sense to spend the time finding the most perfect combinations that you can. Open your eyes to all its possibilities and you will have endless fun layering up each room that you decorate.

57

OPPOSITE This serene blue-and grey colour scheme has been given a jolt with exuberant Bloomsbury-inspired fabrics on antique French chairs. Early 20th-century paintings and a modern uplighter make a bridge between past and present.

WORKING WITH COLOUR

The advantage of finding that all-important anchor piece is that you then have something around which to create a scheme. It is much easier to work in this way than to design a yellow room, for example, and then try to find good pieces of furniture to fit. The anchor piece may well combine many different colours, particularly if it is a painting or a carpet, so do not feel that you will be over-restricted at this creative stage.

Look carefully at the colours within the surface. Using colour well demands a confident approach, so remember that you are looking for ways to accentuate the importance of your chosen focal point, not to play it down. There are essentially three directions you can choose to go.

The first is to build the scheme around the notion of sympathetic colours. These are colours that have the same tonal value. You have to imagine lining up a row of coloured pencils – perhaps a grey, blue, yellow, pink and cream. None of them dominates; yet all the colours seem to blend in together. Let us imagine that you wish to create a blue room around the distressed painted surface of a grey-and-giltwood chair with faded blue upholstery. That does not necessarily mean only using blue, it could be about choosing shades that complement the ones in the furniture and then using the blue in the largest proportions. If you tried to create a scheme using blue alone, you might well be in danger of swamping the very piece that you are trying to highlight.

The beauty of working with tonal value is that you can put any colour with any other colour and it will work. What matters is making sure that the depth of colour remains the same. You cannot, for example, hope that a soft powder blue will work with sage green or mustard. But a denim blue could

POSITE When creating a
ourful display, as with the
sses on this decorative
okcase, think carefully
out the effect of different
ckdrops. These
ligraphied vellum
cuments are an unexpected
t successful way of keeping
e eye focused on colour,
ile introducing an under-
rrent of additional interest.

LEFT Allow one colour to
dominate when thinking about
collections. Here a group of
Cranberry and clear glass
19th-century vases make a
pleasing display when set
against the light. The heavy
Paisley curtains pick out the
colours and make a foil for the
slight variations in shade.

look wonderful with these muddy colours. Often when you study a piece of furniture, you realize that the maker has embraced the idea of complementary colours – all you now have to do is translate it into the room itself.

The second way of approaching colour is to use ones that come from the same family. The red family, for example, might have crimson at its centre but in one direction moves towards oranges and browns and in the other towards pinks and purples. The blue family might stretch from those same purples right across to turquoise and the beginning of the green family. Here it is not tonal value that is relevant, so much as using a colour to its full potential by selecting only shades that are in some ways related.

Let us return to the idea of creating a blue room around the French armoire. The second way of doing so would be to layer up many different blues

within the room, perhaps using the ones at the very edge of the boundary – purple, for example – as accents. An accent colour or highlight plays exactly the same part in a colour scheme as a bright scarf would against a black suit: it creates an element of visual interest without detracting from the effect as a whole. This decorative technique can be particularly effective when you are working with very bold colours such as red.

The third, and bravest, direction to go in would be to work with contrasting shades. Here the idea is to create an element of surprise – so that you give someone a jolt as they walk into a room. Clashing colours are an extreme version of this, but using them requires confidence. Contrasting colours are an accepted tool within interior decorating, and have a particular relevance in contemporary interiors. Imagine the cool blue room you created above using related shades, now imagine the impact

of bright orange upholstery within that setting. It is the vibration between the blue and the orange that creates the drama.

Neutrals, pastels and vivids

There are certain combinations of colour that are in widespread use today. The first is the neutral collection: these can be used in any setting from a small country cottage to a loft-style apartment, but tend to give a contemporary look. That does not mean to say they have no relevance to antiques. Nineteenth-century Chinese furniture, for example, which is very sleek in form can look wonderful in such a Zen-like, no-colour environment.

Pastels have also made a come-back in recent years, but are not so insipid as they once were. At one time this family was essentially white with a tiny amount of colour added. Now it is the opposite: bright colour with white poured in – giving the same effect as pouring cream over a blackberry tart. New pastels can look wonderful with distressed painted finishes and other soft-coloured furniture.

Vivid colours are those that are brilliant in hue. They are the sort that have full-on, heart-stopping impact when you walk into a room. Interestingly, they have an important place in the history of decoration – Chinese yellows, imperial reds, emerald greens and dramatic blacks provide a

LEFT Blue-and-white is a classic colour combination th continues to have a relevanc This 18th-and 19th-century kitchenware has a surprising contemporary look, proving that although it may have be around for centuries, its appe shows no sign of fading yet.

brilliant canvas on which to work. Vibrant colours can create the most stunning backdrop for collections or important pieces of furniture. Always go a notch braver than you intended: you will be surprised at how quickly you acclimatize to the saturation of intense colour.

Historical shades

In recent years, there has been a growing demand for historical colours, and paint manufacturers have been swift to meet this demand, although some have done so with more integrity than others. They tend to be quite muddy colours, which are perfect to use in northern light.

Paint was mainly mixed from local earths and coloured with iron oxides or copper compounds. Interestingly, this palette changed very little for 500 years. Because of this, some colours were found only in certain geographical locations – the way of making the paint hardly varied, but the earths and pigments available did. One of the reasons why conservationists would like us to look kindly on historical shades is that they are often look so sympathetic to the landscape.

Historical shades embrace the idea of tonal value – they often work together very well. Try at least to consider banishing brilliant white from your home. This is a twentieth-century invention, which is so stark that it kills more subtle colours close to it.

You should differentiate though between modern paints that mimic historical shades and those that are made to traditional methods. If you have a period home, you should always choose the latter because they allow the fabric of old buildings to breathe properly, allowing damp to evaporate into the atmosphere. Modern paints often have a plastic coating which seals walls and can eventually be harmful to period properties.

Traditionally made paints are also environmentally friendly compared to modern ones; the latter derive from the plastics industry and contain petroleum. But perhaps most important of all to the would-be decorator – they quite simply look better. Aesthetically, they hold the edge because they have far greater intensity than standard colours.

RIGHT The boldness of newly manufactured pieces can make a pleasing contrast to older faded ones. Blue, white and green are the key ingredients in this basement kitchen but English pottery is teamed with modern Greek designs to dynamic effect.

BOTTOM RIGHT Think about how patterns, as well as colours, are repeated within a room.

That is not to say they should be confined to traditional interiors. Their visual impact means they can also work well in very modern settings. After all, a 300-year-old house was at the cutting edge of architecture in its day. It is time to blur the edges between traditional and modern.

Specialist paint finishes

It is no coincidence that the vogue for traditional colours has come in tandem with a revival of centuries-old paint techniques. Distressed wall surfaces, which have depth and texture, are now to be found in every fashion-conscious home. These are an excellent way of introducing colour, particularly if you are still weaning yourself off safe creams, because it is a way of breaking down a strong shade.

Think back to the subtle variations that would be found within that painted giltwood chair. To surround it with bold flat colour would not do it justice. How much better to complement it with a colourwash or a distemper finish: something that echoes the imperfect surface. But the walls should always play second fiddle to what is within them or hanging on them, unless you want to highlight them. It is not as if paint is the only option, although

POSITE: The base for this ulent red and green colour heme was the 19th-century igler carpet, which looks ignificent teamed with an th-century red Italian velvet dspread. A fragment from a th-century Brussels tapestry ngs over the French nguedoc marble fireplace.

ABOVE A dramatic backdrop was needed for this pair of hand-coloured engravings, showing *The Drunkenness of Hercules, Bacchus and Ariadne* by Angelo Campaneli, *circa* 1802. The occasional table by Thomas Hope, holds an Empire bronze lamp which completes the classical theme and has the functional use of showing colours at their best by night.

it is certainly one of the most versatile. Wallpaper is also making a come-back, so keep your eyes open for increasingly exciting and pleasing collections. Lining walls with fabric is another way of introducing texture.

Lighting

Using colour effectively also means making sure that a room is well lit, at all times. Unsympathetic

*O*ne good period piece makes a huge difference because the whole room
pivots on it. In this sense, antiques set the tone of a room through
patina, depth or colour. The craftmanship also gives enjoyment, which
is why it is lovely to restore something. An antique has already had so
many lives, so it is satisfying to give it a new one.

NINA CAMPBELL

lighting will make any room appear deadened.
When selecting colours, you should always live with
them first so that you can study how they change
through the day and when artificially lit.

What is important is to design a lighting scheme
that is as flexible as possible. You need task lighting
for activities such as reading, working, applying
make-up or cooking. Ambient lighting changes the
mood of a room, and this in turn needs to reflect the
change from winter to summer or day to night. But
directional lighting is also essential for focusing
attention on a specific item – a picture light can be
positioned above a painting, an uplighter below a
statue or a row of mini spots above a collection of
objects. You can also use directional lighting on
particular pieces of furniture, such as the one you
have chosen to be your anchor piece.

Lighting is so fundamental that it cannot be added
later. Ensuring that power sockets, light switches
and cables are in the right place means careful
planning before other parts of the decorating scheme
are considered. Lighting is guaranteed to show the
colours you choose to the best advantage, and so, by
association, everything that is displayed within the
room. Make sure it is right from the word go and
everything else will fall into place.

RIGHT Different shades of the
same colour can be used to
build up an atmoshpheric
scheme. Genevieve Weaver's
narrow dining room is a
symphony of blues, from the
woad and indigo stripes on
the walls to the collection of
English and Chinese-export jars
on the table. Reflected in the
mirrored panels can be seen a
collection of antique blue-and-
white drainers hung in
corresponding lines.

Chapter 6 Texture *and* Pattern

LEFT Textures work well when teamed with their opposites – think of ways of teaming matt with gloss or rough with smooth in your own home. These simple boxes and baskets from rural China are coveted by designers today because of the textural feel of the weave. Here a tartan throw provides a pleasing contrast.

OPPOSITE Pattern can be used to provide a visual link between different styles of furniture. This brick design was copied from a fresco in the Provençale Abbaye. It makes an interesting foil to the Venetian mirror and Anglo-Indian chaise longue. The mosaic Provençale console table, made from broken pieces of porcelain, also adds interesting texture.

TEXTURE IS BY FAR THE MOST IMPORTANT DESIGN story of the last few years. Not that there is anything new about it; antiques are a wealth of textural contrast as a walk around any antique shop will signify. The difference is that decorators are now shifting the focus away from colour and pattern and onto texture itself. They are building up schemes around key pieces, such as the distressed surface of a 200-year-old table, and juxtaposing these with objects that have a contrasting feel. It might be that metal is placed near splintered wood, so that the gloss of one is accentuated by the dullness of the other. Or perhaps curtains in ravishingly fine silk will be hung next to a Roman blind made of coarse hessian or tweed, so the different attributes of each are emphasized. It is a very effective approach, particularly in a room where colour has been subdued.

71

RIGHT This harmonious group
of objects sets a tone of
sophisticated simplicity. The
rough ridged linen vase has a
sculptural quality which is
echoed in the shape of gourds
and other dried fruits. The
silver Han vase and bamboo
table also reflect the linear feel
of the assembled objects.

OPPOSITE The eye takes
pleasure from making links
from one object to the next.
Here a pair of fine Regency
decanters stand on black, re
and gold coasters. These pic
up the texture on the basket-
weave vase next to them,
although in origin they are
separated both by time and
distance.

In recent years designers have inundated us with chenilles, velvets, satins, sheers, faux furs and other sensuous materials. Often their inspiration has come directly from the past. Look to antique textiles for heavyweight tapestries, luxurious silks, intricate embroidery, floaty organzas or crunchy taffetas. But of course texture is about more than the fabrics in a room. Wood veneers, metals, glass, stone, ceramics and leather are just a few of the textural choices you can make when choosing furniture.

Naturally, antiques have an enormous relevance here. It is often their surface texture which makes them so beautiful. A metal-and-marble console table which has rusted over the years should be left well alone because the rust has become part of its character. The patina that builds up on pots or dishes over centuries should never be cleaned away; it is part of their history. The cloudy effect around the silvering of mirrors is similarly to be treasured

not destroyed. Antiques should look their age; it is what sets them apart from modern reproductions.

That is not to say you should not look after those things you buy. Some objects, such as silver or glass, should be cleaned so that they gleam and sparkle. But you must learn to differentiate between everyday dirt which should be removed and the imperfections caused by the ageing process itself. The latter have an intrinsic beauty which has been recognized by decorators only fairly recently.

USING TEXTURE

As with pattern, the first thing is to decide how you want to use texture in your own home. The contemporary approach is to place the spotlight, sometimes literally, on the anchor piece and then build up contrasting textures around it. So it might be that you have one fabulous piece of furniture, such as a French gilt-and-marble console table from

*I*t is fantastic to take something very elaborate and decorative but extremely distressed, and place it in a sparse minimalist interior. You will find it sings. No matter how good a reproduction might be, you never achieve that textural quality with anything but the real thing. it is something you can't explain; it is just there.

JOHN MINSHAW

Above: A drape of fabric softens the lines of the room around it – here a 17th-century embroidered Spanish silk brings a sensuality to this corner of a drawing room. Antique textiles are a wonderfully effective, and often inexpensive,way of bringing a textural dimension into a room.

LEFT An enormous 18th-century Flemish tapestry depicting biblical scenes dominates this harmonious drawing room. Its texture brings a depth to the rooom that a flat canvas could rarely achieve. The carpet is Aubusson and sets the tone for the other colours used in the room.

the eighteenth century, and that you then want to create some visual excitement by keeping everything else in the room very plain and understated in order to accentuate its opulence.

Another way of working would be to build up a whole wealth of texture within the room, just as you might use colour. This would result in a maximalist look, as opposed to a minimalist one. Just imagine sumptuous fabrics, such as silks, velvets, satins, taffeta, fur, tapestry and ribbons, all combined together to produce a really extravagant mood. Curtains, cushions, throws and upholstery could be the starting points. Now imagine introducing rich woods, gilt frames, oriental rugs, chandeliers, flowers and scent. This layered look is far removed from the more contemporary one, but exploits texture just as dramatically.

A third possibility is to choose textures that complement the centrepiece. For example, you might choose a wall finish that echoes the surface of a piece of furniture. Imagine the distressed surface of an antique elm table against indigo and cream hessian walls, for example. Or the impact of mirrored walls on a highly polished piece of Chinese lacquered furniture.

The mistake is to design a scheme around too-similar textures. Think of some conventionally fitted kitchens and you have an idea of what can go

75

wrong – all those wood units with wood worktops and wood floors result in a very boring look. It is no wonder that designers are waking up to the fact that an injection of granite, marble or stainless steel can make all the difference to the final look.

Texture and mood

The more aware you become of texture, the more you will realize what a very important part it has to play in your decorating scheme. Not only can it bring a feeling of depth and interest into a room, but it can also be used to send out messages about the sort of mood you want to convey.

If you need convincing, think about the materials you wear: contrast, for example, the feeling of a silk and taffeta ball dress with the simplicity of a cotton T-shirt; or the heavy wool of a man's suit with the gossamer lightness of a satin camisole. Textiles are very sensuous and are key elements in conveying messages about how we feel. You can use them in your home to achieve a similar task. Not that creating an atmosphere is confined to what fabrics you use. The grain of a certain type of wood, the pitted surface of stone, the lustre of metal, the folds that form in leather – all of these can play a part in building up a decorative look that is both aesthetically pleasing and which touches a deeper nerve about the sort of person you are. It is well documented how colour emphasizes and influences our moods; texture takes the idea one step further.

One of the joys about buying antiques is that so many of the materials they incorporate are now unavailable because they have such a rarity value. This applies not only to certain exotic animal skins, horns or shells, but also to woods that are now seldom harvested or stones that cannot be mined.

There is no longer the free trade around the world that once existed; customs laws quite rightly protect the cultural fabric of once-exploited countries. And much of the craftsmanship that once produced truly exquisite work has long since died because of the lack of interest. All of this increases the appeal of antiques and antiquities, because they encompass within them a rich vein of social history – a direct link with a way of living that has often ceased to exist. It is this that gives them such relevance in the eyes of designers today.

OPPOSITE Keep pattern simple in a small room. This tiny dressing room has been lined with inexpensive blue-and-white striped fabric in order to give interest and definition. It also serves a functional purpose as there would barely be room for cupboard doors to swing open. A 19th-century campaign bed provides an interesting focal point.

LEFT The fabric pulls back to reveal shoes and other items of dress which have been stored away. A pattern with thin stripes, as used here, make a room appear taller than it actually is. Had conventional fitted wardrobes been used, the room's atmosphere would have been far more claustrophobic.

THE IMPORTANCE OF PATTERN

It is easy to forget that other essential ingredient: pattern. Yet pattern lies at the very heart of decoration. Flat colours on their own cannot give a room depth, character and vigour.

Certain patterns are reminiscent of specific locations or cultures, and this, too, can be consciously exploited. Tartan, for example, can never be separated from Scotland. Its effect in a room is always to make it appear warm, cosy and cocooned from the elements. Romantic florals are the epitome of Englishness – they introduce an atmosphere of tradition, serenity and a breath of country air. The Greek key pattern is used to express a mood that is classic, elegant and rather intellectual. Paisleys have a more bohemian, well-travelled and comfortable feel. Toile du jouy is pretty, feminine and chaste. When choosing patterns, it is important to have an idea of what they signify, so that you can choose

ones that are in keeping both with your home and your possessions. This will also help you to avoid those that you think are too clichéd.

One of the reasons why people have become nervous of using pattern in recent years is that the over-coordinated look has become unfashionable. Pattern is essential in decoration, but coordinated ranges make rooms appear dull and lifeless. If you are nervous about using pattern, then don't introduce too much at once. Better to have only one or two patterns, but to use them boldly. This doesn't necessarily mean wall pattern of course, it could be included in a sumptuous carpet, a magnificent pair of curtains, or a stunning collection of china.

Using pattern

There are two ways of using pattern: looking at what you own and reflecting the patterns that are already there; or imposing pattern on a room to achieve a

79

LEFT Pattern can be both synthetic or natural, as this collection of Victorian tea caddies shows. Some are made of antique tortoiseshell, while others are crafted from parquetry of exotic woods, yet together they make a sumptuous display. The close juxtaposition gives them even more impact.

OPPOSITE Three-dimensional objects have a tactile quality, which is why this French 17th century carved marble portrait has such power. Sculpted by Jean Hardy, it shows the Emperor Augustus. The classic reference is echoed by the 2000-year-old Apollonian vase

particular effect. Both are acceptable, but the looks they create will be very different. The former is almost organic in its approach. The second is more traditional. Both recognize that pattern can be a powerful force in decoration.

For example, if you have a room that is imperfect in its size, proportions or shape, then you can use pattern to disguise its faults. Just as using an over-scaled anchor piece can actually make a room appear bigger, so can very bold pattern. If you use a fiddly pattern in a small room, it will just emphasize how tiny it is. But if you have the confidence to scale pattern up, the eye will be drawn to the largeness of the scale rather than the measurements of the room. If you want to draw the eye towards the most pleasing aspect of a room and away from dead corners, then again use pattern to attract the eye and don't use any in the spaces which you want to become almost invisible. If you have a most

beautiful outlook, then play down pattern at the window so that people see the view rather than looking at the curtains.

Pattern can also be used, like colour, to draw together certain elements in a room. Take a look at the decorative features in the room where you are now. List the motifs on furniture, fabrics and floor that are already there. Don't just include the obvious, look closely at inlays on furniture, ornamentation on china, the curve of door handles, the weave of rugs. Now consider whether there is one pattern here that you would like to have prominence over the others. If so, this might be your cue to use it as an echo throughout the scheme. This needn't necessarily mean using it in an aggressive way; you can take the subtle approach and still achieve a very dramatic effect.

Wall pattern

Pattern on walls has the biggest impact of all. This is because it surrounds you in a room, and gives the impression of enveloping you within it. Because of this, bold pattern, like strong colour, is not for the faint-hearted. It is exciting, stimulating and absolutely uncompromising. You need to make sure that the other ingredients in a room, such as furniture and floors, are imposing enough to counteract its dominating effect.

OPPOSITE Think creatively when choosing a wall covering. The hand-written vellum indentures which have been used to cover these bathroom walls achieve a patterned effect which gives the room enormous interest. Aged tortoiseshell mirror and green frogs bring in sympathetic colours.

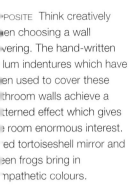

LEFT You can create pattern through display as well as decoration. This collection of antique measures and mathematical tools has been carefully arranged to geometric effect. The Han vase in the foreground has a textural tone which is in keeping with the surrounding objects.

Wallpaper has a perennial appeal and has proved to be one of the most exciting areas in design. For those who want to create a period look, perhaps inspired by William Morris or A.W.N. Pugin, the time could not be better. There are wonderful authentic reproductions of old designs available, often copied from small fragments found in old country houses. And, even better, some companies produce them to their original scale – which means very large indeed. The so-called traditional designs of a few years ago tended to miss the point because they were so scaled down for modern houses that they lost all their impact and significance. There is now a recognition among wallpaper designers that size really does matter.

Reproductions are only one side of the story though. Wallpaper is an exciting tool in the hands of contemporary designers, so be prepared for some really innovative ranges to make an appearance. The textures within these can make a wonderful backdrop for key pieces of furniture or well displayed collections.

Not that this means the end for paint. Specialist paint techniques are still growing in popularity, but the trend is towards making them more exciting and sophisticated. Paint enthusiasts are now more likely to tackle the complexities of Italian plaster stucco or faux lacquering than be content with cutting out a stencil or using découpage techniques. The subtle look of colourwashing, dragging and sponging is giving way to applied decoration. This might take the form of geometrical patterns painted onto walls, for example, or metallic stripes replacing dados. But don't get carried away: walls should always be a backdrop to furniture, not the key ingredient. The best advice is to keep a sense of perspective when using wall pattern and don't allow it to dominate your scheme.

Chapter 7 Collections *and* Display

OPPOSITE Collections can be used to enhance the nature of a room, as with the display of items that was bought specifically for this music room. Attention to detailing counts: note the lyre motif in the Georgian chairs, which is then reflected in the pair of paintings and also the candelabra above.

LEFT A macabre and very unusual Russian carved skeleton chair, *circa* 1890, sets the morbid tone in this library. It was sent by a jilted lover to his beloved on her wedding day. Coffin covers, embalming bottles and other sinister objects accentuate the mood. Fine paintings by both Magritte and Chagall help to punctuate the more eccentric curiosities.

THERE ARE FEW BETTER WAYS OF BRINGING immediate interest and character into a room than through a collection of some description. Collections send out a message about the sort of person you are – they can describe your interests, your travels, your priorities and your aesthetic judgement. This in turn means they provide the ideal conversation point for visitors. Not surprisingly, they are often housed in dining rooms or living rooms – the public spaces of a house – because of this. Aesthetically, they are also successful. A mediocre object will take on new depth if you have enough of its relations. One ancient bottle of thick greenish glass has very little appeal, but put it with 40 others and you are making a design statement. Now take this idea a step further and think about where to house these bottles for maximum attention, how to light them well and

85

OPPOSITE Here creamware
has spilled over into a
neighbouring simulated
bamboo bookcase dating fro[m]
early Victorian times. In a
maximalist interior like this or[e]
such contrived clutter
enhances the atmosphere. I[n]
more purist one, it is importa[nt]
to keep editing a collection
according to the space.

RIGHT One of the golden rules
of displaying collections is that
if you have it, flaunt it. One
piece of 18th-century English
creamware is not going to
have an impact within a room,
but a hundred pieces will.
Such a display needs very little
in the way of a backdrop – this
simple Welsh dresser more
than suffices.

how to arrange them to give the whole group a more sophisticated edge. The result: a focal point. Individually, the components of this focal point are unassuming, rather uninteresting glass bottles. But with some skill and a clever eye, you have made the whole a hundred times more interesting than the sum of its parts.

Not surprisingly, collections have a long and respected history in the world of decoration. They have always represented the intellect, taste and wealth of the person they belong to – and certainly this notion has never completely died away. However, the emphasis on design today is more on simplicity than opulence; artisan craftsmanship rather than fine materials. This means that collections today are as likely to be garden tools or battered leather trunks as silver tea spoons or Spode creamers. This diversity has opened up all sorts of possibilities for decorators. Collections have become a way of revitalizing dead spaces, providing focus, or bringing in a layer of character to a room where none existed before.

How to collect

There are two ways of approaching the business of collecting. The first is to build up a collection painstakingly slowly over many years, taking enormous pleasure in each new acquisition. The

*U*se strong colour and rich texture to create a pleasant background
which will bring the beauty of the object 'en valeur'.
Pattern can be too intrusive, the idea is to focus the eye on paintings,
antique furniture and works of art rather than to distract it.

MADAME CHARMAT

LEFT This grandly decorated gentleman's study has become an ode to Napoleon, with a myriad objects that relate to the emperor's life from paintings of his battles and portraits of his generals to ivory miniatures showing him with Josephine. Collections are usually grouped together but this one is dispersed throughout the room making it possible to discover something new at each turn.

second is to buy a collection complete, not so much out of enjoyment of the individual pieces as with a mind to the decorative effect of the whole ensemble.

The joy of buying an instant collection is that it will have an immediate effect within your home. For those without the time or inclination to build up a display, this can be the answer. What many people want is the immediate impact of a display, be it small-scale decorative objects, such as tortoiseshell boxes, ormolu frames or jewelled hat pins, or the larger scale dynamics of huge olive oil jars, oriental straw baskets or croquet mallets.

You have to decide for yourself which type of collector you are. If you have a pet passion for a particular type of china, such as eighteenth-century creamware for example, then you may find that half the pleasure is in scouring sale rooms and antique shops looking for pieces that you are missing. You will probably also enjoy learning more about the subject with each new addition that you buy. The collection as a whole will give you enormous pleasure, but you are likely to be fascinated by one or two much-loved pieces.

Amateur collectors often become passionate enthusiasts, and before too long have joined the experts in that particular field. As the depth of their knowledge increases, they often become more critical of the first pieces they bought and become

89

This collection of early 20th-century paintings, including one by Paul Nash, looks best grouped together for maximum effect. Below them is an 18th-century painted bookcase with cast-iron grille, while more contemporary furniture emphasizes the innovative nature of the pictures.

OPPOSITE An eye-catching group of four cameo paintings (part of a set of eight) by Christoph Unterberger, 1732–1798, painted *en grisaille* and depicting various gods makes a stunning focal point to this cool, modernist room. The clean lines of the Italian armchair in the foreground is perfectly in keeping with the look.

more choosy in what they buy next. The opposite end of the scale is looking at collections purely from a decorative point of view. There is no doubt that they bring character into a room, as well as visual excitement. The beauty of collections as design ingredients is that they allow you to turn anything into a focal point so long as you multiply it. Because it is the aesthetics that count, rather than the quality, you can also mix in sympathetic new items with old.

WALL DISPLAY

Many people find arranging a group of objects on a wall the most difficult task of all. It doesn't matter whether they are pictures or three-dimensional items, they often appear to be hung without any regard to aesthetics or order at all. Take paintings for example. If you have eight pictures, then don't spread them throughout the room by hanging two on each wall. This will simply emphasize the big

expanses of space between each one. Instead arrange the eight pictures together and leave the other three walls blank. The eye will immediately be drawn towards the group and not towards the bareness of the other walls.

If you have quite a large collection of paintings, start by laying them on the floor and moving them around until you are happy with the overall look. As a general rule, the larger ones should be hung lower than the smaller ones. But whether you choose an effect that is more random than symmetrical is very much a matter of personal taste and depends on what suits the character of the room. Your eye should tell you when the proportions of a group work and when they do not. Once you have an effect you like, make a plan reminding you of what goes where and measure the distances between each picture. Hang the central one first and then hang the others, working outwards and upwards from this.

OPPOSITE There is nothing haphazard about this arrangement. Vellum books, modern galvanized metal boxes and other acquisitions are beautifully arranged in a fine 19th-century Indian cupboard. Such a discipline requires a well trained eye.

RIGHT Another example of casual but contrived. Here blue-and-white 18th and 19th-century Chinese kitchenware takes pride of place on modern industrial shelving. The message is clear: aesthetics has its place, but function is also important. These objects are still in use as they have always been.

If you are hanging something three-dimensional on the wall, perhaps a collection of straw hats or china tureen lids, then you should follow the same method. However, this time you need to be influenced by how well certain colours or shapes work together. Take the example of blue and white drainers (see page 69). There is a surprising amount of variation within the family known as blue and white. The first task is to make sure that the chosen drainers complement each other well: blues that are too green or whites that are too white can be immediately rejected. Secondly, assess their shapes, whether they are oval or round, in order to achieve a symmetrical effect. It is important to include nothing that will affect the look.

Don't forget, too, that framing is not just limited to pictures – old menu cards, sheet music, match-boxes and antique textiles are just a few examples of objects that can benefit from being framed. Not only does it increase their aesthetic value, but it also means they are well protected behind glass. Good framing is an art, so don't attempt to cut corners unless you're confident in your own skills. Find a framer who is sympathetic to your possessions and can bring sound advice to choices concerning mounts, frames and glass. He or she can make the world of difference to the finished result that ends up hanging on your wall.

DISPLAYING COLLECTIONS

A collection that is scattered throughout a house is of no use whatsoever in terms of design – although it can also be said that a home filled to bursting point will never look boring. When using collections decoratively, the first rule is to bring all the collection together into one area so that the sheer numbers have an impact. Having said that, you may need to edit it. Sometimes collections grow out of all proportion; they begin to dominate the room they are in so completely that they become overwhelming rather than aesthetically pleasing. You do need to consider this. It is not a question of

93

RIGHT If you have invested in something you really love, it is worth spending a little more making sure it is well displayed. These Han dynasty stick men are over 2,000 years old. Here they have been given military order by being placed on custom-made wall-hung plinths which bring them up to eye level.

OPPOSITE A Han dynasty unglazed horse is supported on a transparent Perspex plin, which makes it look as thoug it is suspended in the air. The strong textures and simple forms of the vellum trunk and silver-glazed jar accentuate th rich patina of its aged surface on which some of the original paint still remains.

putting all a collection on view to make a display. It is a question of choosing things from it to make a good display.

That means being disciplined. You have to accept you cannot necessarily include every item. Some things might be better being packed away or being used to make a secondary collection elsewhere – perhaps on a landing or in a bathroom. Alternatively, they could even be sold with any money made being used to buy better pieces.

The only way to assess a collection aesthetically is to lay it all out in front of you on the floor, and to look not just at the individual charm of certain pieces but at how shapes, colours and textures within the group complement and contrast with

each other. A quite mediocre example might be worth including because of the dynamics it creates when it is juxtaposed with something else. A better quality piece might have to be discarded because it is not strong enough when placed within the collection as a whole. The size of the collection will naturally be determined by where you are planning to house it.

Depending on what the collection comprises, it may be kept in a specially acquired piece of furniture – such as a dresser for china or a display cabinet for pocket watches. Or you may decide to have something specially built for it, such as an alcove with shelves for ivory figures or marquetry boxes. Perhaps you intend the collection to be

94

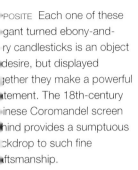

OPPOSITE Each one of these elegant turned ebony-and-ivory candlesticks is an object of desire, but displayed together they make a powerful statement. The 18th-century Chinese Coromandel screen behind provides a sumptuous backdrop to such fine craftsmanship.

LEFT Treen is a generic term for small antique wooden objects, like the arrangement shown here. The beauty of the natural material combined with the skill of fashioning such pieces is what makes this display so covetable. Lignum vitae, out of which these are made, is a rare dense wood with distinctive markings in the grain.

displayed on a wall or arranged on the surface of a table. When making your decision, you should consider how best it will be seen as you walk through the door. You might consider that it is more important to see it when you are sitting down. Look at the room and decide if there is an area that needs an extra boost. Collections are an excellent way of lifting otherwise dull spaces, so make sure that yours works for you.

Consider practicalities too. Do you need to protect your collection from small fingers or curious pets? If so, perhaps you should place it at as high a level as possible. Will it need protecting from sunlight by being placed behind glass or being situated in a dark corner of the room? If so, glass should be non-reflective so that it does not mar the enjoyment of the collection itself.

Of course it may be that the collection has been bought for a particular piece of furniture. Anchor

pieces, such as huge dressers or armoires, only take on full effect when they are properly dressed. It is worth considering this when buying a major item and allowing for it within your budget. You must determine whether the collection is there in a supporting role to something else within the room, or whether it is itself the star turn.

Having decided where your collection is going to go and how it is to be displayed, you should now consider extra ways of giving it visual impact. Take a walk around a museum or art gallery to pick up ways of doing this effectively. Colour, for example, is a wonderful tool. You could paint a display alcove in a stronger colour to the rest of the room as this immediately draws the eye towards this area. Choose a backdrop that complements the shades within your collection without dominating it.

Good lighting is also a must. Lighting is so atmospheric that it immediately creates another

97

layer of interest, and gives even more significance to the group of objects you have chosen to display so decoratively. If you are having furniture or shelves built for display purposes, you should always specify integrated lighting within them.

Height is another factor. Specially commissioned plinths or stands can be well worth the money as they have the effect not only of lifting the objects to the most advantageous height, but also giving them more significance by sending out the subliminal message that such attention to detailing means this group is of particular importance.

Don't allow any other object nearby to detract from the overall effect of the collection. If, for example, you have carefully arranged a display of magnifying glasses on a side table, then make sure nothing else is put down on it – even temporarily – that spoils the overall effect.

Finally, make sure you maintain your collection to the highest standards. There is nothing desirable about tarnished silver or grimy teapots. Collections are about creating drama – a theatrical flourish that lifts the whole scheme – so you must make sure that nothing spoils the magic.

OPPOSITE One of the joys of
collecting is that you don't
have to have a particular
reason for doing so – it is just
a way of expressing your
delight in something. This
horde of lions is part of a
collection that includes Roman
pieces from two centuries BC
through to Victorian and later.

RIGHT Lions have become
such a passion for this owner
that they are displayed all over
the house, including on this
charming Gothic chiffonier.
They are made of many
different materials, including
terracotta, wood, bronze, iron
and porcelain. Individually
charming, *en masse* they
look stunning.

Chapter 8 Mixing *Styles*

OPPOSITE This chrome armchair and table from the 1920s is an ideal companion to the sleek 18th-century Chinese Huang Hua-Li sideboard made from indigenous hardwood. Thousands of miles and hundreds of years separate the two periods, but similarities in size and form mean they correspond visually.

LEFT If you have the confidence, you can blend many different styles together within one small space. Here a French 1920s' sculpture and a primitive-style birdcage sit easily together. An 18th-century chair has been painted red and covered with appliqued fabric to inject a note of drama.

THE WONDERFUL THING ABOUT DECORATING today is that there are no rules. People no longer feel that they must opt for a particular style – be it Edwardian, Art Deco, 1950s or minimalist – and keep to it rigidly. Anything goes in today's homes and that is why they are so fresh, original and interesting compared to those of 20 years ago.

Of course it takes courage to go your own way. But happily more and more people are doing just

that. There was once a feeling that styles could clash, just as colours or patterns might. But look back through history and you soon see what nonsense that idea is – after all, only the exceptionally wealthy bought new furniture for fashion's sake a hundred years ago or more. Furniture was something that was passed on from generation to generation and only replaced when it had to be. That means that all homes were at one time a

*D*ecorating is not about creating a historic cameo. Antiques are often a bridge between what you want to do as a designer and the building within which you are working. New interiors and architecture can talk to each other through antiques.

CHESTER JONES

mixture of styles, so there is nothing new in the idea of eclectic. Linens were darned, cooking utensils mended, chairs repaired, curtains remade: thrift was always the key word. When the affluent classes of the eighteenth century began to travel and acquire objects from abroad, they did not throw out their entire possessions to accommodate their latest finds. Instead their new treasures, whether they were Ming vases, Grecian busts or Indian chintzes, were given pride of a place in their homes sharing space with all their other more commonplace goods. So those people who love the eclectic look today are only reflecting the way that their ancestors once chose to live.

If you look in the dictionary, you will find that eclecticism is the notion of borrowing freely from many different sources or doctrines. Certainly freedom is the key word. Those who mix styles with confidence and sophistication are able to do so because they are not cowed by any notions of: 'Will it go?' or 'What will other people think?'. They are able to see beyond the age of a piece and instead focus on its shape, form, colour or texture. These attributes decide how it will sit with other objects in a room.

There should always be space for objects you love in your home, no matter how unusual they are. Teaming modern pieces with antique ones often

RIGHT Chinese furniture is often so classical in form that it can be integrated into any style of interior, as this table shows. This grand hallway also boasts a Cambrai 18th-century tapestry, French 1930s' armchairs and a 20th-century Indian cotton dhurrie, yet the effect is as though it has been this way for centuries.

LEFT It is possible to create a frisson by introducing furniture styles that are unexpected in certain interiors. Here a very purist, almost minimalist, home with bare walls and loosely dressed windows has a French Regency chair placed centre stage. The eye is drawn to the purity of the piece rather than its age.

brings out the best in both, as they take on even more significance and interest when partnered with something very different in style. Contrast can be far more stimulating and exciting than harmony. If you have a very bold piece of modern art, there are few better ways to draw attention to it than to hang it in a very traditional room. On the other hand, if you have a fabulous 200-year-old table, then why not team it with a set of modern leather-and-stainless-steel dining chairs so that each design ingredient is given maximum attention?

This impact is not restricted to the notion of mixing periods of furniture together. It is a very global approach, because it allows you to trawl for objects from around the world. China, India, Thailand, Vietnam, Singapore, Arabia, Egypt, Mexico and other cultures have all had a tremendous influence on western decorating. Europe itself has been a huge melting pot of ideas and inspirations. It is perfectly acceptable to introduce Chinese lacquered furniture into the pared-down simplicity of a very architectural space, or to place heavy colonial furniture in the nooks and crannies of a country cottage. Not only do you have the whole of human history to take ideas from, but the whole of geography as well.

The beauty of designing rooms eclectically is that it is a look that can suit any period of home, from a loft-style city apartment to a classically proportioned Georgian house. It has a classic timelessness that shows no sign of dating yet – unlike the vogue for choosing only one period from which to decorate a house. It particularly suits those with a low boredom threshold because objects can be discarded or introduced with ease. And it encourages the eye to become more sophisticated, as you become attuned to looking at different styles and assessing the chemistry between them.

OPPOSITE Antiques can add an unexpected twist to very modern settings. This state-of-the-art swimming pool room has a classical theme, as the trompe l'oeil frieze below the ceiling shows. A pair of Victorian cast-iron Atheniennes are sympathetic to this, providing a focal point in an otherwise understated space.

LEFT Choose objects, either contemporary or antique, with clean lines and they will work together very well. These French empire marble-and-bronze tazzas are carefully juxtaposed with slender sophisticated lamps and modern glass-topped furniture. The effect is confident and urbane.

THE ROLE OF HISTORY

It seems extraordinary that the word eclectic should have taken on such significance in the last 20 years. The concept of eclecticism has been around for nearly four centuries, so why should it have been reinvented comparatively recently?

To understand why mixing different design styles works means taking a look back through the history of interior design, and in particular to Europe's long-standing relationship with China – or Cathay as it was once known. It was the Portuguese who first established a formal diplomatic foothold there in the sixteenth century, and began trading in fabulous goods such as porcelain, silk and tea. It is said that even tea chests were lacquered, and that it was these that first gave European furniture designers the idea for making lacquered furniture. The success of Portugal's trade with Cathay paid rich dividends. It was not long before Lisbon was the wealthiest city in Europe.

Queen Elizabeth 1 of England took a dim view of the Portuguese success. In 1600, she granted a royal charter to the newly formed East India Company giving it a monopoly on trade with India and the Far East. It didn't take long before fabulous cargoes of fine fabrics, wallpapers, lacquered furniture, gold and silver ornaments, pottery and spices were being unloaded from docks in Britain, France and

107

Right A pair of turn-of-the-century French leather armchairs sit happily next to a Chinese lacquered cabinet, sharing as they do a slightly reflective surface. Modern paintings often look dramatic when placed next to traditional furniture – this bold abstract is by Neil McLean Robertson.

Opposite Introduce a jolt of surprise. A chrome-and-leather armchair by Marcel Breuer makes an interesting clash against an elaborate giltwood console table and forces the eye to explore both forms. The Impressionist painting introduces a third dissenting note, but the whole effect is stimulating and exciting.

Holland. By the second half of the seventeenth century, European nations were gripped by a frenzied craze for anything oriental. No sooner had a ship arrived, then it was stripped bare by our design-conscious ancestors.

As with all fashions, demand soon outstripped supply. This was the period when the Chinese began to manufacture all kinds of furniture, paintings and accessories specifically for the western market. Chinoiserie was born – that peculiar infant born of western desire and Chinese exploitation. It never seemed to occur to Europeans that Chinese people did not themselves own bookcases, waste paper bins or writing desks. All that mattered were that these objects came with the required amount of lacquer and bamboo.

It followed that the next step would be for European craftsmen to begin manufacturing similar pieces in the Chinese style, first sending wood to Cathay to be lacquered. Who cared that these designs were haphazard? Large petalled flowers, flocks of exotic birds and robed mandarins were foreign enough to fool western customers.

But that wasn't the end of the Chinese story. Chinoiserie was reborn during the mid-eighteenth century when the baroque style declined. It suited the pretty romanticism of rococo, when natural motifs such as shells, waves and monkeys came to the fore.

The twentieth century was no less influenced by China, India and other eastern cultures than the previous ones. In fact, in some ways its influence could be considered more profound as western culture also welcomed and embraced eastern philosophy as much as its decorative style. Popular taste moved from highly decorative and ornate objects to ones with a chic and simple style. Today, those objects that were once owned by the humblest

LEFT This pool ante-room (see page 106) has a strong classical theme apparent in the plaques, busts and urns – mostly marble and gilt bronze – that are displayed within its walls. The side tables are hand-painted faux marble, and make an interesting contrast against American leather sofas, which have been introduced for contrast and for comfort.

RIGHT A bold contemporary work of art is an unexpected, but dynamic, focal point in an otherwise traditional dining room. Sheraton chairs, a pedestal table and an early 18th-century gilded and faux marble table bring gravitas to the scheme. The bronze figures introduce another layer of interest.

peasant now seem to be imbued with a charm that designers here fight to emulate.

Perhaps the greatest change to the way we live over the past 30 years has been how well travelled we have become. As airline prices have dropped, our expectations about what a holiday should encompass have risen. It is no longer unusual for people to visit Africa, Australia, India, Hong Kong and many other far-flung locations.

Above: This magnificent ebony cabinet with drop silver handles dating from the 19th century is the setting for sleek Grand Tour black slate obelisks of the same period.

One of the joys of being on holiday is shopping, so not surprisingly our homes are often bulging with exotic wares which we take pride in displaying. But because we are so much more aware now about how things look, we often try to buy goods that will make a statement when we bring them home. It is not enough to just have a souvenir. Today we want to place something centre stage that will send out a message not just about where we have been, but about the sort of people we are.

The Grand Tour

It was the same for the more wealthy of our forefathers. They discovered the lure of the Grand Tour back in the eighteenth century, but the only difference then was the lack of rules about customs and exchange rates so that there were no limits on what they could bring back, other than of the practical sort. Columns, huge statues, plinths, busts, obelisks and other antiquities were transported from the streets of Greece, Italy and Egypt to satisfy the Georgian craze for neoclassicism. Our equivalent obsession today would be rugs from Pakistan, baskets from Vietnam, candlesticks from India or silk paintings from Sri Lanka. The better travelled we become, the more we learn. Buying new is often not good enough, what we really want is a slice of that country's history to call our own. This makes global

Global travel has had an enormous impact on the visual arts, interior design, fashion, cookery – in fact on just about every area that encompasses the word 'lifestyle'. This in turn has enabled us to become far more visually literate, so that good design is now central to the way we experience the world.

You only have to look at shop windows, restaurants, advertising, magazines, book jackets and children's clothes to see how revolutionary a change there has been. It is impossible to see how this would have come about without travel becoming more accessible.

LEFT Take pleasure in setting up
stylistic contrasts, such as this over-
elaborate single Bagues wall sconce
hung over a spartan Directoire side
table. Such opposites bring a touch of
wit to a room. A line of creamware
provides a visual barrier between
the two.

OPPOSITE Asymmetry can b
an effective tool when
decorating, particularly whe
pulling together a number o
period styles. Here it reflects
the contrasts between fine
furniture and distressed oak
between sombre 17th-centu
Spanish oils and a turn-of-
the-century circus clown.

antiques hot news. So it is clear that the idea of mixing styles is nothing new. For centuries, furniture was passed on through the generations. But at periodic intervals, it would be added to so that the whole look was often a mix of periods, styles and materials. It was a very twentieth-century approach to reject all those hand-me-downs and instead furnish houses from scratch often with cheap, badly made furniture.

All this means that when analysing the eclectic look it is important to put it into context. It is not a new idea, it is in fact the cornerstone of European design, which has borrowed from other civilizations and eras to take on the significance it has today.

MIXING STYLES IN A ROOM

The most ordinary space can be transformed by what is within it. The beauty of eclecticism is that it offers interest and excitement, so it is unsurprising

that it is such a perennially successful look. It is not a difficult style to master, although there are certain pitfalls to avoid. The main thing is to train your eye to appreciate the intrinsic beauty in objects from many different cultures and periods. Look for strength of form, quality of craftsmanship, interesting combinations of materials, colour and surface texture. Avoid pieces that are so over-stylized that they will intrude, rather than attract. Don't cram too much into a space: it is better to have one or two important pieces and build around these, rather than introducing a very mixed selection. Above all, learn the importance of positioning items within a room for maximum impact. You need surprisingly few pieces to achieve a global feel; what counts is how they react together.

Have the confidence to trust your own taste and instincts. The success of this look centres on surrounding yourself with furniture and decorative objects that are in some way personal to you. The whole point of eclecticism is to end up with something original and stimulating. It would be missing the point entirely to try to copy the look as seen in a shop or a magazine. Have fun with it: loosen up a little. Mixing styles is an admission that we are changeable, imperfect, humorous, curious and above all, human. It is these qualities that give this style its edge and brilliance.

Chapter 9
Variations *of* Style

ONCE THE CORE DECISIONS HAVE BEEN TAKEN concerning the decoration of a room, you must turn your mind to another essential ingredient: ambience. One of the advantages of using antiques as the basis for a scheme is that they are perfect for introducing mood, personality and originality into a room. They are such a personal choice that they immediately send out messages not just about your taste, but about you as an individual.

Many leading decorators use antiques to bring wit, beauty or drama to a room. This applies to cool contemporary interiors as much as those based around a period look. The reasons are obvious: many antique objects are hand-crafted and so unique in form, texture or decoration. Many are of a scale that is out of kilter with our modern homes, but which give them enormous aesthetic impact. Many were made long ago when certain materials, now rare, were commonplace. All these things combine to give them a desirability, which few modern manufactured objects have. What often appeals to decorators is the juxtaposition of new with old – the visual frisson which a well chosen antique can bring to a scheme.

LEFT Antiques have the potential to take you down many stylistic paths. Do not confuse this with recreating a pastiche of the past. Instead look for ways of expressing your individuality and creativity through the juxtaposition of favourite things – both old and new, simple and elaborate.

Magical Maximalism

FORGET THE OLD ADAGE THAT LESS IS MORE. IN THE maximalist interior, more is more. Don't assume for a moment, though, that achieving this look means overfilling the room, without regard to style or quality. The maximalist eye is as discerning and true as the minimalist's, but understands how to build up layers of beauty and interest within a room through an astounding quantity of objects. Designer Ann Mollo, whose home is shown here, is passionate about the warmth that antique objects can bring to a room.

This sort of contrived clutter is perfect for collectors who really love the things they own. It takes years of dedicated buying to bring to fruition, unless you are prepared to pay for instant collections. Individually the objects have integrity and value.

This look is a celebration of beauty and craftsmanship – it imbues a joyous feeling to anyone walking in. Happily it can suit town or country homes, large or small areas, house or apartment. However, it is very rooted in a period setting so would not be ideal for a modern loft or town-house.

OPPOSITE Maximalists are skilled at creating different niches around their homes for adored treasures. This wall is covered mainly with pictures of animals. The Gothic trellis screen was salvaged from a summer house.

ABOVE This 1960s' table by George Ciancimino is the best of its period. It is beautifully dressed with 18th-century creamware and candle holders from an Italian church.

Maximalists do not need to worry too much about the architectural bones of a room or improving proportions or aspect because the impact comes from the articles on display. Decoratively, rooms can be kept simple – natural floorcoverings are best; historic paint shades are perfect on the walls; while lashings of inexpensive fabric can be used to dress the windows.

The idea is to create a warm, comfortable cocoon into which furniture, books, pictures, ornaments, china and all manner of decorative fripperies can elbow each other out the way for attention. Not that

119

RIGHT Focal points are important in such crowded rooms. This turn-of-the-century portrait of a deer hound in chalk and pencil is so loved by the owner that it takes pride of place on an easel. To one side is a painted early 19th-century glazed bookcase.

OPPOSITE Mix styles with confidence. A portrait of a collector: this painting of Ann Mollo and her dog looks perfectly at ease among the furniture and objects she is passionate about. The statue is early 16th-century and was originally of George and the Dragon; the chairs were made for a Georgian grotto; and the black chiffonier is an example of primitive chinoiserie.

there is anything vain about possessing so much – part of the maximalist charm is that value is played down. Dressers bulge with china; bookcases sag under the weight of books; walls disappear beneath paintings – the exuberance of the look works not because the maximalist is keen to show off what he or she has, but interestingly because there is a feeling that things do not matter so much that they can't be used.

AN INDIVIDUAL APPROACH

This style is about as far from the museum-like antiques-must-be-revered approach as possible. The message behind the maximalist room is that enjoying life is what matters, and that to end up with a home like this means that you lead a very interesting and fulfilled life already.

Individuality and a certain amount of quirkiness are key to this approach. There are often very personal stories behind possessions –the furniture has often been inherited from a much loved member of the family. The maximalist always treasures much of what he or she owns because of these important, former connections.

Maximalists have enormous vision. When they buy a piece of furniture, they understand exactly how it should be dressed for maximum drama. They are the stylists of the antiques' world. That means they understand perfectly how to mix objects in terms of colour, style, texture and form. They think carefully about display, whether it be with a bank of paintings on a wall or a collection of *objets d'art* on a table, and take great pains to make it appear as if an effect has been arrived at almost by accident, when in fact it was very carefully planned.

If you really love antiques and have no wish to continually edit down what you own, then this look may well be the one for you.

Gracious Grandeur

THERE ARE SOME HOMES YOU WALK INTO WHERE everything is absolutely as it should be. There is an atmosphere of gracious living which can be achieved only through the combination of a generous budget and excellent taste. The style is grand, but not so ostentatious that it is alienating. It often has quite an international flavour, reminiscent of diplomatic circles, and so it is a look that is immediately identifiable be it in Paris or California.

International decorators such as Madame Charmat, David A. Harte or Renoir Designs are

ABOVE The richness of this hallway, with its elaborate parquetry floor, is echoed in the colours of an 18th-century tapestry. Formality is evident in the positioning of the gilded Marquises chairs, *circa* 1835.

LEFT An oversized Ionic capital table of carved wood dominates this city snug. Wood panelling is perfect for winter, while in the summer the door opens into the garden. On the mantel is a collection of newel post knobs.

OPPOSITE The beautiful marble fireplace is the focal point in this classically designed sitting room. The symmetry of the room has been emphasized with the positioning of sofas, side tables and 18th-century lamps at each side of it. The Greek key pattern on the table accentuates the classic approach.

skilled at achieving this look. First you must begin with rooms that are beautifully proportioned with a wealth of architectural details. There needs to be a feeling of space, so double dividing doors that open onto more rooms are an asset. Ceiling roses, cornicing and architraving should all be as decorative as possible. A good aspect is also a boon.

Quality is the motivating factor here. Floors will be thickly carpeted, and the carpets themselves might be fairly decorative with custom-made

ABOVE A portrait of the Duc de Maine dominates this formal drawing room. The chairs are part of a 19th-century suite, but have been gessoed and gilded in recent years. The upholstery stripe is a silk satin in deep colours which emphasizes the grand feeling of order. To the right a late 18th-century over-mantel mirror adds more opulence.

borders and central designs. Fireplaces are likely to be made of stone or marble. Walls will almost certainly be papered, again with quite an ornate design. Windows will be dressed in sumptuous silks and other luxurious fabrics. This style is almost presidential in its grandeur – in fact there is something comforting about using such blue chip ingredients to achieve the required resonance.

Naturally enough, antique furniture is very much a part of this look. It tends to be the best of its type

RIGHT This perfectly proportioned
panelled room promises leisurely
dinners of the finest calibre. Its elegant
symmetry has been accentuated by the
placing of the furniture, which includes
French Empire fruitwood chairs, and
the immaculate attention to detailing in
the table settings. The impressive
chandelier over the table is Russian
from the nineteenth century.

RIGHT This perfectly proportioned panelled room promises leisurely dinners of the finest calibre. Its elegant symmetry has been accentuated by the placing of the furniture, which includes French Empire fruitwood chairs, and the immaculate attention to detailing in the table settings. The impressive chandelier over the table is Russian from the nineteenth century.

in period style and quality. What counts is the wood, when it was made, the maker, the finish and the ornamentation. A grand setting is not the right one for unusual or quirky pieces of furniture. Nothing should be allowed to unbalance the effect.

HISTORICAL LINKS

However, that does not mean to say that this look is rigid. It is certainly allowable to juxtapose a modern work of art with a seventeenth-century console table, for example. What is important is that both are the best of their type. There are some styles, such as Art Deco and Napoleonic, which are so strong that they do not mix well with others, but usually the grand look recognizes that rooms should be a bringing together of design references from the past. To decorate a room in one period style would be very dull indeed. This approach is all about making strong links with history, which give a room a feeling of permanence. Antiques also have the advantage of holding their value, and those who favour the grand look often like the notion that their money is reasonably safe. They also appreciate the links with the past that antiques give them.

This applies not just to furniture, but to paintings, silverware, china, glasses, decorative collections and other objects. The grand style needs a lot of layers within a room, because the spaces themselves are so large. Walls, surfaces and shelves must be filled with the appropriate items. And these in turn must be of the appropriate quality, so that nothing jars. However, it is rather an impersonal atmosphere. These are, in effect, public rooms owned by people to whom public face is important. Grand is about sending out the right messages, rather than inviting people to take a glimpse of the private you.

People who choose the grand style tend to have the financial means to support it. This is important because presentation is key and there is a lot to maintain. Highly polished surfaces, spotless floors and perfectly plumped upholstery are all part of the success of the look. It is no surprise that the quite different, rather bohemian style, of faded grandeur came about through the English aristocracy no longer having the means to maintain their possessions properly. The grand look bears no more resemblance to the faded one as a Chanel suit does to a flea market find.

Poetic Purism

IMAGINE SITTING DOWN TO WRITE A LOVE LETTER, but first having to find the most perfect hand-blocked creamy paper imaginable. The purist room is like that piece of paper. Once you have the blank sheet, then you are ready to write using the most exquisite calligraphic script imaginable.

Purism can also be described as architectural, but should never be confused with minimalism. It is far softer and more sensual than the latter as designer John Minshaw – the man behind this serene interior – shows. It does not demand that your possessions be pared down to the absolute minimum. However, it does mean thinking carefully about what you possess and editing accordingly. The idea is that attention should be focused only on those things that are of aesthetic value. Less unattractive possessions should be cleverly concealed or discarded altogether. It is a disciplined, ordered look, which architects and designers increasingly embrace with a passion.

The framework of the room itself is crucial to the purist. The ceilings, walls, windows, doors and architectural details must all be assessed first. If the proportions are not good, then a new space might well have to be carved out of the old – this is why this look is sometimes described as architectural. The framework is the canvas on which the purist works, so it is vital that this is right.

OPPOSITE Absolute harmony and simplicity are what matter here. This modern checkerboard floor is perfect for a purist scheme, with an early 19th-century carved marble relief resting informally against the wall.

ABOVE The neoclassical style dominates in this well planned, sophisticated study. It is unlikely to date and so is perfect for the construction of new furniture in this architecturally rich space.

Then comes the question of looking at the functional aspect of the room and concealing cables, light switches or any other ugly essentials. Radiators are allowed only if they have some aesthetic merit, such as the appeal of old cast iron ones. Televisions and music system will also need to be hidden away – perhaps in a particularly beautiful custom-made cabinet. Good lighting should also be installed, to highlight the one or two pieces that really matter.

RIGHT This Egypt-inspired bathroom has columns made from ash inlaid with boxwood and tulip. The mirror is also a modern design, but the eyecatching bronze figure dates from the Vienna Succession, 1910, and is made in the Egyptian style. Soft colours and carefully positioned lighting have been planned to unify this calm scheme.

OPPOSITE A magnificent 18th century French mirror dominates one end of this simple, serene drawing room. The focus is on the 19th-century bronze statuette and the small gilt frames, which are 18th-century Venetian. On the floor are a mixture of jars from Spanish Art Deco to Wedgwood kilnware and striated contemporary design.

Decoratively, it is a question of combining simplicity with quality. Floors can be kept plain but beautiful: wood block or stone are ideal in the purist interior. If windows are architecturally pleasing and enjoy a good aspect, they can be left undressed; if privacy is a problem, then the simplest window treatment should be considered. Walls too should not embrace colour or pattern as these are too provocative. A subtly textured surface is allowable, although absolutely plain is best.

It follows then that strict criteria will be in place for furniture and decorative objects. Purists judge each piece on its merits, be it old or new. What counts are clean lines, quality of materials, interesting surfaces and scale. Antiques are an integral part of this; they bring a patina and refinement to a room which purists adore. So, a classic marble fireplace might be adorned with nothing more than a large gilt mirror, but the mirror needs to be the most perfect of its kind. Or a Regency chair may be placed in front of a window, where its shape, upholstery and style will all combine to turn it into a design statement.

AN EXACTING EYE

Purists favour a little over a lot – large scale over small. Overscaling is a well recognized way of shaking up the dynamics of a room to interesting effect. Symmetry also plays its part in emphasizing the dedicated approach behind the design. Immaculate still-life arrangements are carefully contrived to heighten the visual pleasure as you look round a room. Purists have such an exact eye that everything they position in a space immediately takes on new relevance.

You can't decide to be a purist: you are born one or not. It is about having a vision and refusing to compromise. When done well it is beautiful.

ABOVE Many people assume that there is no place for antiques in the kitchen because of its functional aspect. In fact these industrial iron Singer stools made in the 1920s sit happily with the sleek fitted furniture around them.

Unexpected
Urban

Cities are a melting pot of cultures, and this is what makes living in them so stimulating and exciting. There is a particular style of decorating which reflects the confidence, exuberance and individuality of urban living today. It takes references from many different sources and mixes them altogether to create a feeling of surprise in a room. Once described as eclectic style, it has now out-grown that tag and become more sophisticated and sharp.

Central to the urban philosophy is the idea of mixing styles – blending eastern with western; old with new; simple with stylized; primitive with elaborate. Urban is not constrained by notions of 'will it go?'. It can see the potential in many objects that would be rejected by the grand, the purist or the connoisseur. In fact the success of the urban look is partly down to the fact that you will find things here that would not be seen elsewhere, often partnered by the unexpected.

Urban style tends to have quite a hard edge to it, and is almost masculine in style. Floors are often stone – slate or limestone are particularly good

LEFT An Indian four-poster bed dating, from the 19th century, makes a dramatic focal point in this master bedroom. The faux leopard-skin bedspread adds a witty touch.

OPPOSITE This chic aluminiur wine rack started life as an A Deco baker's rack, but has been renovated to blend wel with the 1930s' dining suite.

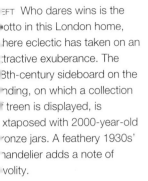

LEFT Who dares wins is the motto in this London home, where eclectic has taken on an attractive exuberance. The 18th-century sideboard on the landing, on which a collection of treen is displayed, is juxtaposed with 2000-year-old bronze jars. A feathery 1930s' chandelier adds a note of frivolity.

LEFT The flexibility of urban style can be used to draw attention away from awkward proportions, as with this guest bedroom set into the eaves. Green Han dynasty jars and tortoiseshell objects – including a handsome mirror – provide a focus for the eye. The Dutch, walnut, 18th-century armchair makes a pleasing centrepiece.

choices. The walls are usually plain, but have a hint of colour in them. Blinds are often chosen for windows because of the need for privacy. Sofas and chairs tend to be big and roomy because comfort is high on the urban priority list.

COMBINE WITH CONFIDENCE

An anchor piece is as likely to be a glass-and-metal Italian, seventies' table as a Jacobean sideboard. What counts is the size, form and texture of a piece, and the impact it is going to make within a room. Urban has enormous wit; it enjoys the friction caused by placing objects near to each other which have no obvious common ground. So a modern work of art might be hung above a traditional piece of furniture; or a very pretty chair might be placed next to a dark, heavy chest. In the urban world, opposites attract. Good use is made of every available space, including dead corners up the stairs or along landings. Space is at a premium in cities, so it should never be wasted – there will always be something that fits the required space.

Because the emphasis here is on making a strong statement within a room, quality is not so important as individuality. It is possible to achieve the urban look on a fairly tight budget, and some styles and periods of antiques can still be bought fairly inexpensively. The trick is to look closely at objects that other people are not interested in, and see if they have the design potential this look requires.

Finally, keep moving along. Urban should never be allowed to stagnate; what keeps it looking fresh and original is the opportunity it offers to keep metamorphosing into something else. It has a chameleon quality which makes it very attractive to those with a low boredom threshold.

Lavishly Layered

OPPOSITE A gloriously witty touch is apparent here which shows this decorator's ingenious eye. A portrait of Alidad by Victor Edelestein takes the role of a mirror – if you sit on this richly covered sofa you will see the view that the portrait reflects. The walls are painted with patterns based on Islamic motifs.

THE LAYERED LOOK IS DRAMATIC, THEATRICAL AND sumptuous – one that Alidad has very much made his own. When done well, it is the most seductive style that you can imagine. There is something almost decadent about its indulgence and luxuriousness.

Happily, it is not essential to own a large period home in order to make this style work. It can be just as effective in a small, modern space. But you will have to be prepared to cheat by adding in decorative cornicing, fireplaces and ceiling roses before starting.

Lighting is key to this look, so before you begin make sure that you have the flexibility for a variety of lighting effects. Televisions, music systems and similar equipment will need to be concealed. You could consider commissioning a decorative armoire or cabinet to house these in. You want to end up with a room which is functional and beautiful.

Once you have sorted out the basics, you need to turn your mind to the decorative. Layering means adding ornamentation to every surface imaginable – floors, walls, even ceilings. Think rich colours, eastern carpets, magnificent and elaborate curtain treatments, splendid upholstery. But remember – this is only the beginning.

It is not enough to choose a fabulous fabric for the sofa. You then have to add in gorgeously-coloured throws, cushions and bolsters. These in turn must

ABOVE AND RIGHT Each part of this elegant room is dressed for effect. The 19th-century, Gothic desk is balanced by well placed lavender topiary and a bronze head. Antique remnants draw the eye to the sofa.

OPPOSITE It is difficult to imagine a more sumptuous mood than is to be found in this golden dining room. Layering means building up the style with glittering glass and candlelight, rather than toning down. The stamped leather walls are made by Lidad Ltd, but use a 16th-century design which is then distressed to look aged.

LEFT Another luxurious still life which shows the decorative value of of attending to detail, even in the most unassuming of corners. The antique tablecloth and wall panel set the tone – books, bronzes, busts and other treasured objects are then built up into a pleasing tableau.

be embellished, tasselled and trimmed. The trims have to be the most lavish you can find. Imagine laying a table for dinner. The layered look demands nothing less than a setting worthy of a Bacchanalian feast. Think about including glasses of burnished gold, fine china, night-scented flowers and an army of candles. Why settle for one of something when 20 would do just as well?

EXTRAVAGANCE RULES

The joy of the layered look is that it makes the visitor feel as if he or she has walked into the pages of a novel or onto a film set. It is escapist and exciting, but that does not mean it is all top show. Because the basics are firmly in place at the beginning, these rooms work from a functional point of view as well. But what makes them feel so wonderful to be in is the extravagant attention to detail that they have.

Antique furniture and accessories are an integral part of this look. They bring a patina to a room, which is in keeping with the textural approach. And stylistically they fit well because the emphasis is on tradition and comfort. Antique textiles in particular are an asset here. In fact, fabrics are so important to rooms like these because floors and furniture should feel swathed.

Display is also important. A block of paintings on the wall or a collection of curios arranged on a table are all part of the layered feeling. There is often a sense of symmetry in how such things are arranged, but nothing too rigid. Above all, this style is intensely comfortable. It gives the sense of cocooning you in fabric and colour; creating a warm, sensual sanctuary far away from the cold, dangerous world outside. Embrace the lavishly layered look and the chances are that you will never want to set foot outside again.

137

Connoisseur
Calibre

THERE ARE ONLY A FEW ANTIQUE COLLECTORS WHO have both the wealth to indulge themselves at whim, and the taste to make that whim worthwhile. These are the connoisseurs. It is worth looking at their style – even though so few of us can afford to emulate it – because it is the rarest to achieve.

The connoisseur has a deep love for antiques – perhaps he or she was brought up with them from childhood. This love transformed itself into a passion early in life, and with that came an insatiable desire to know more about certain types of antiques. Connoisseurs can afford to buy the best of whatever they choose, but would never rely on other people to tell them what it is. Instead, they devour books on the subject, eventually learning so much that they may even publish some well-regarded titles of their own.

The discipline with which they buy pieces is ferocious. Only the best will do – but that does not necessarily mean the most expensive. Because they learn so much as they buy, they often find bargains and take enormous pleasure in paying less than they should for certain objects. However, they would also pay well above the going rate to take possession of an object they considered key to their collection.

Connoisseurs favour classically decorated houses, as these provide the perfect backdrop for their possessions. Expect to find elegantly

ABOVE One of a pair, this superb Roman console table in this collector's home is made of carved giltwood and black marble veneer; it displays a melange of bronze, marble and ivory objects. The alabaster urn is 17th-century; the bronze busts are 18th-century, as are the ivory candlesticks.

OPPOSITE This fine Regency mahogany bookcase with a pull-down screen showing a map of 18th-century Asia is rare enough to take pride of place in this connoisseur's city townhouse. It was originally made for the directors of the East India Company. The sofa is Victorian, while the pair of oval Irish mirrors are again Regency.

BELOW These 19th-century Italian marmo rosso marble columns are copies of ancient Roman ruins. Brought back from the Grand Tour, they make a stimulating collection.

RIGHT Chinese 18th-century painted clay figures, all with nodding heads, make a friendly group on this Carrara marble fireplace. Made purely for decoration, they are now rare and very collectible. The overmantel mirror is English and dates from the late 18th century.

OPPOSITE: The mahogany and brass-inlay sideboard and pedestals in this dramatic and luxurious dining room are a rare Regency set. The dining table, with unusual ormolu base, is also Regency, as are the chairs and convex mirrors. Early 17th-century, lacquered Buddhas and an oil painting by Johan Wenzel Peter complete the scene.

proportioned rooms, woodblock floors, fine carpets, strongly coloured walls, elaborate window treatments and comfortable furniture. Wealth does not mean pointless ostentation, which the connoisseur despises. Walk into his or her home and it is unlikely that you would immediately spot the items of greatest value. In fact that is the whole point: part of the pleasure of being a connoisseur is that you appreciate the quality in things which most people are ignorant of and might well overlook when buying. That means they have respect only for other connoisseurs who know as much as them about certain fields of antiques.

It may take money to be a true connoisseur, but that is not the driving force. These people really love and appreciate the things they have, often choosing to bequeath them to museums or art galleries rather than see them passed on to members of the family who might not value them so much.

BUILDING UP KNOWLEDGE

The art of display is important, as connoisseurs like to feel surrounded by their objects of beauty and craftsmanship. Collections are arranged like still lifes throughout the house; paintings are well lit; furniture is always beautifully dressed. There is a confidence that comes from exquisitely good taste.

Don't despair if this description leaves you envious and dissatisfied. We can all become connoisseurs if we are prepared to work at it. There are plenty of areas of antiques that still offer potential to those who want to become serious collectors, but who are constrained by budget at present. Remember that it is not enough to collect one thing; you also have to make it your own. That means learning a lot about it, so that you can be sure you are buying the best. As your knowledge moves into other areas, you will be surprised at how convincingly you too earn the tag of connoisseur.

Unadorned
Understatement

RIGHT: Mirrored doors at each side of the fireplace set up interesting vistas throughout this sitting room. The original distressed painted finish of the Regency sofa breaks up an otherwise clean interior, bringing in a layer of textural interest to the scheme.

LEFT It is easier to mix antiques into a modern space if you keep colours as understated and low key as possible. Here the crisp contemporary furniture and paintings are perfectly in harmony with antique pieces, such as this terracotta statue of Napoleon.

ONE OF THE PROBLEMS OF HAVING A PASSION FOR antiques is knowing when the moment has come to stop collecting. This sort of pared down approach demands a lot of discipline. It revolves on the idea of continually editing possessions so that the things you do retain take on greater visual impact. Decorator Jonathan Reed has a reputation for persuading clients to edit what they own, so that they can achieve the sort of no-frills simplicity that is seen here.

There are shades of minimalism, but that is an extreme version of this style. Understated is a lot easier to live with than the rigidity of minimalism implies. It may be sparse and simple, but it is by no means spartan.

It is a look that can work well in many different styles of house, but on the whole it is best if architectural features are not too visible. Choose floors, walls and window treatments that are beautiful, but not intrusive. Function is a key word here – this is a style where good design is the root of all – so what counts at the beginning is making sure that the space meets all practical requirements. Think about storage, for example, as there must be places to hide the daily overflow of books, papers and other household paraphernalia.

Consider too the layout of each room. The positioning of furniture is crucial because nothing should be allowed to interrupt the flow of the space. It is also important that rooms work in a practical way for the occupants; the way the furniture is laid out is an integral part of this. The underlying philosophy of such Zen-like simplicity is that you own your possessions – they do not own you. The idea is to create a space that is restful and serene, and which is an antidote to the stresses of modern living. Owning less is a way of reducing the pressures which all material goods bring with them.

It is also a way of ensuring that attention is focused on those things which are visually pleasing, rather than being distracted by all manner of other objects.

Antiques are very often the focal point in such schemes, because they provide a depth and patina which prevents everything becoming too one-dimensional. They are not important because of their age *per se*, but because of this aesthetic quality which age brings. Pieces are chosen because of their scale, form and surface texture – these are the objects which create an excitement within an understated room, and bring the whole thing together. Rarity value is important too – this is not a grand room where the provenance of a piece of furniture is important. An eccentric one-off chair from the 1950s has more design relevance here than a good but ubiquitous Georgian chest-of-drawers.

The juxtaposition of old with new is important too. Very often those who opt for this look prefer modern furniture and contemporary style. Antiques might not be the obvious thing they look for, but when they see the impact of the two together it becomes obvious how strong the combination is and how well the styles complement each other.

144

LEFT This wooden slatted screen is a French 19th-century design. Its curvaceous shape and simple construction is surprisingly modern and helps to make an impact in this plain room.

OPPOSITE Furniture in this balanced drawing room is a mix of custom-made modern designs and antique pieces. A pair of French Art Deco chairs has a planned symmetry that is reflected in the positioning of the lamps and the attractive Spanish Art Deco urns set against the windows.

BELOW Another view of the drawing room opposite shows an 18th-century Irish mirror which never dates. Its classic lines blend well into this sleek architectural style.

ORIGINALITY AND QUALITY

Superb craftsmanship is also appreciated – original designs and quality of manufacturer are two criteria that lovers of the understated look will pay for.

However, it is not a look where displayed collections or other assortments of small-scale items are relevant. As with everything else in these interiors, it is best to choose only one or two major pieces for impact rather than risk unbalancing a room by bringing in too much. It is not so much a question of fitting in the pieces you love, so much as specifically searching for the anchor which will fit a space perfectly. Once a room is complete, it is not easy to keep bringing additional things into it either – you need to edit continually. You must be aware of the room as a whole, rather than the individual pieces within it, whether they are modern or antique. What matters is creating and then maintaining harmony, serenity and absolute integrity.

Futuristic *Fantasy*

LEFT Inside this Andreavich cabinet are Voneche crystal tumblers and champagne flutes, *circa* 1830, complemented by Art Deco decanters and silver-mounted champagne bottles. Increasingly, designers are seeking links between cutting edge and period perfection.

THE JOY OF DECORATING TODAY IS THAT THERE ARE quite simply no boundaries; you can be as individual and non-conformist as you want. What counts are personality and confidence. A home like the one owned by furniture designer Lilli Curtiss bucks all conventions just as her designs do, but works because her exuberant personal style shines through. The message is clear: what matters above all is your personal enjoyment of your space.

There are shades of baroque here, but a far fresher interpretation of that often sombre style. However, its drama and sexiness can be seen in the over-large candlesticks; the sharpness of the chair backs and the red velvet of the upholstery. The contemporary twist comes from the feeling of space between objects and the lavish use of leaf techniques to give furniture and accessories a metallic finish.

When you set about creating your own fantasy interior, you should not worry too much about either the age of the property or its architectural style. This sort of boldness over-rides both those things. A room like this one could be as easily created in a modern town house as in a period setting. However, architectural features should be played down rather than emphasized because you

LEFT This Mirth chess table and Regalia dining chairs have graphic shapes and strong colours which echo those found in baroque furniture. The red and white Anglo-Indian chess set is stained ivory, *circa* 1840. This owner's individual taste creates a satisfying link between historic style and contemporary vision.

OPPOSITE Furniture designer Lilli Curtiss uses 18th-century gilding techniques to make contemporary furniture. However, she also uses antiques to shake up very modern interiors. This fabulous railing and copper-leafed cabinet are her own, while the carved giltwood armchair is from 19th-century Germany.

OPPOSITE This mixture of styles works wonderfullly here. The Regalia armchair and modern metal torso look perfectly at ease with silver-leafed Italian candlesticks from the 18th century. Traditionally such candlesticks were only gilded on one side for display. These were designed to be floor-standing, but take on extra prominence raised to eye height.

ABOVE The key to mixing old and new is to find bold themes, whether in shape or colour. This pair of twisting candlesticks reflects the form of a curvy Edwardian match striker.

do not want anything to impinge on your canvas. Walls, floors and windows, therefore, should be kept as simple as possible. Louvred blinds are ideal because they both shut out the outside world and play down the shape and size of the windows. The polished woodblock floor is also an excellent choice as it as likely to be found in modern houses as old ones. Walls are best kept plain, with only an eighteenth-century-style mirror and the shadows of the louvred shutters to break up the smooth surface.

CONTEMPORARY CONTRASTS

The textural contrasts within the room are very effective – silver leaf with chocolate brown leather, for example, or white gold leaf with burr oak and ebony. Antiques are not an obvious addition to such a contemporary look, but in fact they work extremely well. The match striker by the mirror is just one example – in form and surface texture it is perfectly at ease with the modern two-pronged candlestick next to it. The lustre of eighteenth-century glasses complements the copper-leafed cabinet beautifully. Floor-standing, French, gilded, seventeenth-century candlesticks make ideal companions to the silver-leafed furniture.

When choosing such stylized pieces, it is best not to have too much else going on in a room. This style could not be described as minimalist – it is far too

humorous and quirky for that – but it does have a sparseness which is part of its effect. The attention is drawn first to the dramatic form of the chairs, but is then allowed to take in other touches, such as the water-gilded wooden top of the coffee table or the wire sculpture of an upper torso.

It is an uncompromising approach though. There is one signature in evidence, and it would not be easy to integrate other pieces that did not carry it. The reason it works so well is that all the furniture, be it modern or antique, shares the same textural finish, strong character and theatrical form.

Clever Classic

IF YOU WANT A HOME THAT IS WELCOMING, ORDERED and pleasing to the eye, then the classic style is for you. It is the sort of look that has connotations of being comfortable and relaxed, but is also aesthetically well planned. Although it is reminiscent of large country houses and an aristocratic way of life, it has in fact evolved over the years into something far more tailored and structured as the doyenne of English decorating, Nina Campbell, shows in her own home. Companies such as Sybil Colefax and John Fowler are also masters of this approach.

As always, look first at the architecture of the room. Study the doors, windows, ceiling height, even skirting boards. You might consider replacing too-small skirting boards with deeper ones or having the ceiling cornice altered in order to give more emphasis to the room. Look at the quality of the door furniture too. If it isn't up to scratch, replace it. The success of the classic approach lies in attention to detailing and quality.

Function is important so you must consider power points for lamps, where to position radiators and so forth. The key to a classic feel is the notion of quality of life. That is why it appeals to people with busy lifestyles who want to know that their home can be relied upon to function efficiently.

Now to aesthetics. Everything in a classic room should be well balanced and in proportion. A focal

OPPOSITE A fine *bureau de cylindre* makes an effective centrepoint in this entrance hall. At each side are 17th-century chairs upholstered in antique fabric, while the rug is a stunning Aubusson creation. Grand Tour urns and other decorative *objets* complete the classic aristocratic look.

ABOVE A William IV day-bed punctuates the space between one end of this carefully assembled drawing room and the other. Note the symmetry, of the paired Georgian card tables and the elaborate ormolu wall lights above.

LEFT This detail of the day-bed shown above, highlights the glorious combination of fabrics and tassels. If you are lucky enough to have one fabulous classic piece, it is worth dressing it well.

151

RIGHT This French cocktail
table from the 1930s has pull-
out shelves, which make it a
very functional as well as
aesthetically pleasing piece
that suits the practicality of
classic. In the background is a
gilded wooden armchair, one
of a pair, which dates from
19th-century Italy.

OPPOSITE The lovely blend of
colours in this family sitting
room was inspired by the 18th
century needlework carpet.
Fabrics have been used
lavishly, creating a comfortable
and inviting atmosphere.
Antiques, such as the Regency
convex mirror, give the whole
room the sense of permanence
wanted in this look.

point is a must, and this will usually be a fireplace in a living room, but it could also be a particularly impressive piece of furniture such as a large bookcase. Focal points will be beautifully dressed. So the fireplace will have fire irons, a fender seat, a magnificent mirror hung above, plus a real coal fire.

KEY INGREDIENTS

Because comfort is important, the classic room will be beautifully decorated. It demands thick carpets, tailored windows treatments and elegant wallpaper to set the right note of tradition and elegance.

How the furniture is positioned is also important. Symmetry plays a big part in creating this look. Having said that, it should not be too rigid or the relaxed atmosphere will be lost. However, side

tables, lamps and cushions should all emphasize the sense of order. Pictures too should again be hung in a block for impact. If you have a collection of some sort, then display it together to give it more significance. A classic room may well have a lot of ingredients, and contain books, magazines, flowers, photographs, but the surfaces must always be clean with everything on them perfectly displayed. It is this thin line between comfort and clutter, being relaxed but not too relaxed, that makes the classic look harder to achieve than it may at first appear.

Choose furniture that has strong lines to accentuate the formal layout of these rooms. Think, too, about the importance of scale. Overscaling – the introduction of large pieces into a modest-sized room – helps to give such interiors a real sense of

importance. Huge mirrors, large lamps, plumped-up cushions and tall chairs are some examples of ways to do this.

Antiques are an integral part of the classic interior. This is not only because they emphasize the traditional note within the room, but also because of the materials from which they are made. A fine piece of wooden furniture is a must in these interiors, so bookcases, tables, sideboards and chairs introduce the necessary richness and quality. The patina is an indispensable ingredient of the classic palette.

Antiques also introduce a timelessness which is in tune with this decorative philosophy. They offer reassuring links with the past, which make the future seem less uncertain. Classic interiors feel as if they have always looked that way and will survive unchanged for many years yet.

153

RIGHT Blue-and-white is still one of the most effective ways of injecting colour into a corner of a contemporary room. Complement vases with bright flowers, allowing one shade to dominate.

OPPOSITE The youthful, fresh feel continues with a collection of glassware on open shelves – some antique Whitefriars or Cranberry, some new additions. The vivid geometric upholstery on the 19th-century French, dining chairs adds to the bright contemporary feel.

BELOW A 19th-century, French, wrought iron table looks surprisingly modern when set against bright, sunflower yellow walls. Hung over the table is an ink drawing of the Abbaye de Corneux, which was destroyed in 1792. Below a row of blue-and-white ginger jars echo the linear arrangement.

Colourful
Contemporary

YOUTHFUL, VIGOROUS AND BRIGHT – THESE ARE the adjectives that best describe this breezy, confident look. Ideal for family houses where antiques are used rather than admired, the contemporary style borrows from many different sources and then mixes the whole lot up to magical effect. It follows the philosophy that antiques that have survived this long are clearly a match for young children and boisterous pets, so why worry?

It is a style that can work in all manner of buildings – from modern mews houses to spacious apartments. It accepts the imperfections of a room and works with them, rather than trying to alter them. The idea is to provide focal points for the eye through colour and pattern, which will distract from the less pleasing aspects of a room.

If you do have young children or animals, think practical. Choose hard-wearing floors, paint that can be wiped and robust furniture. Bright colours are wonderful because they lift the spirits as you enter and set the tone for family fun. Plan storage carefully too – child-friendly life flows a lot smoother if there are plenty of places to hide everyday clutter away when evening comes.

Because this style pivots on the idea of breaking down boundaries, it is acceptable to mix in new with old as much as you like. A collection of antique coloured glass can be cleverly boosted with some

OPPOSITE The bold, but comfortable mix of styles in this master bedroom begins with the modern oil painting by Jutrishia Lawlor. Below is a 19th-century, Chinese cabinet in elm, with Han dynasty pottery dating from 2,000 years ago and a pottery grain store of the same age. The bedspread, a 19th-century, French provincial design, has a wonderful lived-in feel .

ABOVE AND LEFT Victorian Cranberry glass has a wonderful colour which adds an exuberant touch to a table laid outside.

modern ones. Victorian chairs might be re-covered in very bold upholstery fabric. To use only contemporary pieces would be rather dull as antiques have a character and depth that bring a space like this alive.

FAMILY LIFESTYLE

When choosing antiques for this sort of lifestyle, there is no point feeling stressed out about keeping them perfect. You must own your possessions, not allow them to own you. If you hate the idea of something being spoilt in any way, you should probably go for pieces that are already distressed. Or simply accept that it is not the end of the world if something picks up some cracks and chips during its stay with you.

Above all, there is a lot to say for the idea of teaching your children to have some respect for the furniture and accessories they share their space with – it is patronizing to assume that all youngsters are wilfully destructive. Try to find the line between asking them to have some regard for the things you own, while not continually nagging at them to be careful. However, don't even attempt this lifestyle if you can't accept that accidents do happen.

Because this look is so eclectic, it is possible to change it as often as you like. The exchange of one anchor piece for another can dramatically alter the mood, even if nearly everything else stays the same. This flexibility is just one of its many strong attractions. Colourful contemporary gives a feeling of lots going on within a room. It creates a contrived busyness which echoes the hustle and bustle of everyday family life – and this emphasizes the character and interest of a home. Both an aesthetic and a functional triumph, it proves once and for all that antiques and family life can be combined to astounding success.

157

OPPOSITE A wonderful ambience is created in this room with this early 19th-century decorated Chinese lacquer cabinet, which makes a fabulous centrepiece. A celebration of decorative styles is evident in the dolphin base of the early 19th-century, German table and the brass-and-leather of the early Victorian adjustable campaign chair.

Chameleon
Charisima

IF YOU ARE AT HEART A SENSUALIST, AN ESCAPIST, a dreamer, then the chameleon look could be the one for you. It is about creating a little piece of perfection; a gilded sanctuary where you can shut out ugly reality and stay safe in a world of your own making. It is not the same as Grand, because the emphasis here is on keeping private rather than going public. Neither should it be confused with Classic, because it is a far more unconventional approach than that implies.

Period architecture is an enormous advantage here: tall sash windows, panelled doors and fine architraving provide the foundations on which you can now build. It is not, however, essential to have big spaces – small ones can be just as effective, so long as you can fit in one handsome anchor piece around which the rest of the scheme can pivot.

Because the chameleon look is based around the idea of fantasy, it should never follow only one style. It is quite acceptable to have early Georgian alongside Art Deco, or Regency juxtaposed with Edwardian. The whole effect should be vaguely period, but at the same time indeterminate. Chameleon takes its name from the fact that a visitor can never quite put his or her finger on what lies at the core of the room.

Because this is a sanctuary, comfort is very important. But money is more likely to be spent on

ABOVE Chameleons appreciate quality in craftsmanship, such as this delightful Sienna marble lamp It is a superb example of carving – Grand Tour style at its most sublime.

LEFT Even the smallest items are chosen with care. These bronze, enamelled paper knives are part of a charming Pierrot collection.

ABOVE Regency pilasters give a built-in bookcase a touch of grandeur. The burr elm bed with ormolu detailing was made by Jean-Jacques Werner in the reign of Charles X and is an unusual addition to a drawing room.

LEFT An amusing and exquisite Pierrot peeps through vellum-bound books.

LEFT Chameleons often spend hours arranging collections of objects. These charming pierrots look as though they have been placed at random, but in fact they have been positioned because there is a connection between each individual's face and a particular literary title.

furniture and furnishings than decor. Floors may be polished woodblock, with fine quality Aubusson carpets that have gone threadbare. Windows can be hung with lashings of inexpensive fabric or antique remnants. Walls are best painted in plain, backdrop colours that can display mirrors, paintings and even empty gilded frames.

However, there should always be one glorious centrepiece, and this in turn should be dressed to the nines. It could be an Empire-style bed, as shown here, or equally well a magnificent painting or a fabulous table. What counts are scale, form and ornamentation. Decorative detail is important, although often this is emphasized by positioning something highly ornate next to something absolutely simple.

Texture is another important ingredient. Chameleons are sensualists, so there is often a feeling of softness and luxury in the materials they choose for their homes. This is not just confined to fabrics: think about the lustre of glassware, the silvering of mirrors, the carved leg of a chair or the plumpness of a bolster pillow. Finding perfection in all of these and in everything else that surrounds them is what motivates these collectors. It is also why display is so important. Hours of planning might be spent on arranging a collection of objects on a table or ensuring that pictures are hung just-so; there should be nothing that offends the eye.

DECORATIVE INTEGRITY

Antiques are naturally integral to this look. It may be possible to cleverly integrate some reproduction pieces into it, but only true antiques have the texture and decorative impact that this style requires.

Chameleons, as their name suggests, are not particularly loyal to their possessions. If they find something that they cannot live without, they will happily sell something else to make way for it. Six months later, they may find that they can live without it after all – and that in turn might be discarded in favour of a new passion. This low boredom threshold is what gives their interiors an edge, because nothing is allowed to stand still for very long at all. The ingenuity lies in their ability to imply the opposite – at first glance, an interior like this looks as though it has been this way for decades.

161

Shoestring *Chic*

OR PEOPLE ON A TIGHT BUDGET, ANTIQUES OFTEN seem an impossible dream. Yet this need not be the case. Like almost anything else you buy, there is an enormously wide price spectrum to choose from – the secret is to buy the best you can but present your objects as if they were ten times the price they really were.

It also makes sense if you spend less on other pieces of furniture, so that you can in effect cream off the extra and put it towards something you really covet. Just buy something basic to sit on, open shelves for cheap storage, plus a few surfaces for books, lamps and other must-haves.

Keep the essentials of the room as plain as possible – floors can just be bare boards or natural floorcoverings; walls can be painted and the windows very simply dressed.

Now the blank canvas is ready for you to introduce some pieces of interest. The rule is to go for quality, not quantity. You could invest your entire budget in one stunning painting, a statue or some other *objet d'art*. It is patina that counts: that

OPPOSITE The natural flooring and plain walls provide a blank canvas on which this dedicated collector can display his treasures. The large vellum trunk to the left is double-hinged with leather corners and is from 19th-century China.

textural quality that is never found in anything really modern. Patina adds class to a room, so choose something with enough surface interest that it brings the rest of the scheme alive.

This could apply to a piece of furniture as much as to a decorative extra. Trunks, for example, are a brilliant investment because they are so functional. They offer both storage and a useful surface, and they often are made in materials which weather beautifully with age. Faded leather and brass with silk lining is a winning combination which looks

163

RIGHT There are some pleasing surprises in this modest bathroom. The basin unit is in fact made from an Indian rosewood sunburst cabinet. Built-in shelves alongside the bath provide an unexpected display area for Han dynasty warrior banner-holders from 2,000 years ago.

good no matter what the setting. Old wooden luggage also introduces a note of faded elegance to a room – there is something wonderfully romantic about antiques associated with travelling; they evoke a sense of glamour and luxury.

AN EYE FOR DISPLAY

The trick when working on a shoestring is to make whatever you own go a very long way indeed. Presentation is all. That means, for example, thinking of the optimum height and position to display something. If, for example, you have a three-dimensional object that you want to display on the wall, you might consider commissioning a plinth to stand it on to give it extra height, and to give it a sense of importance within the room. The effect will be even greater if there are several of these objects and you display them as one block. Stands can also be used to position treasured possessions. Perspex

stands are virtually invisible so that attention is drawn only to the objects themselves.

Juxtaposition is also key. Make the most of the textural qualities of your possessions, whether they are salvaged leather-bound books, ancient stone jars, mathematical instruments or fragments of fossil, by putting them next to or near by other objects of similar aesthetic interest. In other words, it is better to group the few things that you have together for visual impact, rather than disperse them throughout the room where they might become rather lost. This way you create the illusion of having more items than you really do.

The chances are that if you take this approach to begin with, you will soon accumulate treasured objects. Buying on a shoestring budget is where many collectors begin, but is not necessarily where they stay. However, few would part with those early possessions. Buy well now and you will have few regrets later on.

RIGHT This corner of the sitting room shows a small Syrian table made of inlaid wood, ebony and mother-of-pearl. The Chinese bamboo table to the right was a bargain. The owner painted the abstract himself to fill in a bare corner and then placed the English hall bench below, on which are placed simple Indian grain bowls.

LEFT Think laterally when choosing furniture on a budget. These industrial stools salvaged from a factory have been spruced up and now look perfectly at home in a smart kitchen. Breathing new life into pieces is one of the greatest satisfactions of buying secondhand.

165

Chapter 10

Buyer's Guide

RIGHT An early 19th-century, Italian Carrara marble table terminating in paw feet, which shows the quality of marble carving that can be found.

You do not have to be an expert to buy antiques but it does help to have some basic guidelines that you can follow when you are searching for that special piece. This guide gives you some useful information on where to buy an item, what to look for, plus some specific advice on purchasing furniture, porcelain and other items.

WHERE TO BUY

•FROM AN ANTIQUES DEALER – you should be guaranteed peace of mind, if you buy from a dealer, particularly if he or she is well established. Reputable ones will often buy back stock at a later date – although not necessarily at a higher price – or agree to trade it on something. Build up a relationship with a handful of dealers who have the chance to get to know your taste and style. They will then look out for pieces specifically with you in mind and call you when they acquire the right piece. Dealers can also help you acquire some knowledge about the subject you are most interested in.

•ANTIQUES FAIRS – the advantage of these is that you have the chance to study many items from various dealers all under one roof. The disadvantage is that it is expensive for a dealer to take out a stand at a fair, so prices can prove to be high.

•AUCTION HOUSES – these have become increasingly popular with the public in recent years, but they can be difficult places to visit for those who have a limited knowledge of antiques. Not all auctions take place within sale rooms – it is well worth visiting a country house sale where the entire contents of a home from basement to attic are often sold off over the period of a few days. Certainly, you can pick up some bargains, but you can also end up paying way over the odds. So bear in mind the following points:

1 First of all, unlike a shop, it is not possible to take pieces on approval.

ABOVE This fabulous desk from Vizagpatan is a superb example of 18th-century colonial furniture, combining as it does silver, rosewood and ivory.

OPPOSITE Parcel gilt carved wood furniture, French Directorate chairs, Italian mirrors and ormolu-mounted perfume bottles are just some of the lavish selection customers of Guinevere can choose from.

LEFT A Louis XV continental walnut veneer bombé bureau with gilt bronze mounts and handles.

Secondly, photographers are very skilled at making faults disappear for the catalogue. That means you must study an item carefully before bidding for it. You should also look carefully at how it is described. Is there a date for it? Is the word style used? If there is no period or date, it may well be new. If you have specific queries, always ask the auctioneer.

2 Most of the time, price is a reasonable guide in a catalogue. But if a ridiculously low figure is given, beware. You could find yourself enticed to a sale hundreds of miles away and then walk into the sale room and see prices go through the roof. Good pieces make money wherever they are sold, so don't assume you will pick up a bargain.

3 You have to pay a commission on top of the hammer price, so decide on your overall price and stick to it. Read the catalogue carefully to find out whether there are additional costs you are liable for.

•**CLASSIFIED ADS** – these are a very time-consuming way of looking for furniture or other objects because you might have to travel a considerable distance just to see one item. Also you might find it difficult to turn down something, no matter how much you don't want it. It is easier to walk out of a shop empty-handed than from someone's home.

FURNITURE

When you are buying a piece of furniture, first get to know period styles so that you can recognize how old something should be. The big difference between furniture made in the second half of the nineteenth century and that made before is the age of mechanization. Furniture that dates from before 1850 is handmade; sophisticated machinery did not exist at that time but labour was freely available so craftsmanship is often excellent.

ABOVE: A George III black lacquer chiffonier with chinoiserie gilt decoration.
LEFT: This handsome burr elm bed is a fine example of bronze ormolu decoration by Jean-Jacques Werner.

You must look at a piece from all angles, and try and be confident in what you are buying. See if there any obvious repairs that need doing that you have not been told about. Also look to see if anything is out of place. If you do notice something that looks altered or which has been replaced, then ask the seller about it. He or she should at least be able to discuss this.

When you find a piece of furniture that you are interested in buying, and you see woodworm holes, check to see if they are fresh by tapping them. If there is sawdust around them, the woodworm are active and the piece needs treatment immediately.Look underneath and check if any carving is hand-done (i.e. not uniform). See if the veneers are quite thick or if the joints are held together by pegs, also check to see if there is considerable wear on the underside of the feet. If you find that the piece has all these things, then you are either looking at a period piece or a very clever fake. However, if there is a 'no' to one aspect, it means that you are looking at a later piece or one that has been substantially repaired and altered.

This need not matter as a chair of the right style can suit certain interiors where the 'look' over-rides integrity. However, the difference in price means that you want to be sure of what you are buying. The chances are that the connoisseurs among you will want a chair that really was made in 1720 (as with the example below) and not 150 years later. Later copies of furniture rarely interpret the style completely accurately: the carving on the original, for example, will be crisper and the proportions more generous. You need to train yourself to differentiate between the two even without looking for the tell-tale clues.

However, even experts argue about the date of a piece. An amateur collector cannot be expected to authenticate antiques, so always ask the dealer to write down what he or she is selling the antique as – for example: 'A French Louis XV Provençal walnut armchair, *circa* 1750'. This then acts as a guarantee.

CARVED FURNITURE: Look for fluency throughout the piece. Often pieces have been cut down to size and the carving on a stretcher does not match up to the carving on a leg. You may also find that pieces have been married together, and that the top and bottom of a dresser or cabinet did not start life in unison. Look at how well the timbers and the carving match. With a table, look underneath the top to see whether there is evidence of the supporting timbers having been moved. You might notice traces of lines or screw holes (the latter might even have been filled in).

COLONIAL FURNITURE: This furniture is made almost exclusively from hardwoods and ranges from the very finest in style to elaborately carved furniture inlaid with various exotic woods. There are large numbers of late Georgian and Regency-style pieces made from rosewood, mahogany and teak. Influenced by prevalent European styles, these pieces were made using solid timber. The carving on the 19th-century pieces tends to be rougher with an obvious Indian influence relating back to the colonial period. These are considered extremely good value as the timber alone would now be so expensive to buy.

TOP An imposing mahogany Empire table with iron stretchers.

MIDDLE This wrythen fan top table from Ceylon is *circa* 1830.

RIGHT A fruitwood chair from the French Regence period.

Chinese Lacquer: As the sleek lines and slick finishes of Chinese lacquered furniture have proved such an irresistible combination for today's interiors, more and more reproduction pieces are now flooding the market. In fact, the construction of Chinese cabinets and cupboards has not changed in 500 years, up to and including the modern day. One of the more reliable ways of satisfying yourself that you are looking at a period piece is to study the surface patina of the lacquer carefully. Generally, antique pieces have a crackleure – tiny cracks which spread out over the surface of the lacquer – an unevenness caused by it being worn down through the years. When you look at trunks or chests, study the edges from top to bottom. You should see a series of interlocking dovetail joints which, unlike the reproductions, are simply glued. On stripped pine and elm provincial furniture, it is easy to see the raised grain of the wood on the original pieces because they will have suffered years of washing and cleaning which will have worn down the soft wood between the open grain creating a driftwood effect.

Top A Chinese red lacquer trunk – red was the traditional colour given to couples on their wedding day.

Left An early 18th-century Venetian silver leaf mirror. Glass from Murano was prized because of its quality.

Below English creamware from the 18th and 19th centuries has now become highly collectible.

MIRRORS

The glass used in mirrors of 100 years or more begins to show flecks of glitter under the surface, because of the deterioration of the mercury. If you can see what looks like brush marks over sections of the reflective surface, the mirror has been artificially aged.

The frame of the mirror is also important. Don't go for a thin or mean frame. Whether it is gilt, veneered, lacquer or tortoiseshell, make sure the thickness of the frame is in proportion to the frame itself. The only exception might be oval Irish mirrors with glass studs, where the frame is only the thickness of the studs.

PORCELAIN

True porcelain, based on white china clay, is also known as china. It was made in China from the seventh century, but was kept secret from the West until the eighteenth century. An imitator of porcelain was made in smaller numbers, mostly in the sixteenth and seventeenth centuries. Known as 'soft paste porcelain', it was made from white clay and ground glass. Difficult to produce, it is consequently rare in comparison. Production disappeared once the secret of true porcelain was known. Faience is a term now used to describe glazed earthenware popular from the sixteenth century. This pottery was covered in a white glaze to imitate porcelain, then decorated.

Unlike glass, porcelain is very restorable. There are many different levels of restoration, but top quality work is almost impossible to spot. It is only by looking at how light is reflected on the surface that you can see a change. Some people touch porcelain with their teeth, others tap it with a coin to see if it rings true. Both techniques focus on how smooth the surface feels – if it is ridged, that implies repairs have taken place. Be careful when testing as you might end up paying for something you have damaged. Porcelain is so specialized an area that you really should consult a dealer first.

RIGHT This 18th- and 19th-century kitchenware from China was produced for the home market.

BELOW This pair of Austrian urns from the mid-19th century have fine crystal engraving and ormolu work.

GLASS

Although age is not everything, in terms of glassware there is no denying that a pair of Georgian decanters are definitely more desirable than late Victorian copies. Look for a simple shape, with restrained engraving or none at all. The decanter should also feel quite light. Regency decanters are much heavier, with more cutting and engraving but are no less desirable. They should also feature stoppers with matching engraving. Victorian decanters are generally more fussy and complicated with different shapes – the grape-and-vine motif was very popular in this period.

The glass of lead crystal should be a lovely grey colour as opposed to the green or yellow hue of later copies. You should learn what this colour looks like early on, so that you never confuse it with the shade of cheaper glass. It is not to be muddled with rock crystal, also known as quartz. This mineral was used in the eighteenth and nineteenth century often on chandeliers for decoration. It is normally full of striations and looks cracked, but it is much more expensive than glass. The easiest way to tell the difference is to touch it – rock crystal is very cold to the touch because it is a mineral.

Glass can never be restored. You can grind chips out or remake a section, but you can never restore a crack.

Late nineteenth-century and early twentieth-century silver-mounted glass, particularly decanters, are now very collectible. Quite often these are made in the shape of animals or champagne bottles. The Edwardians liked to decant champagne and drink it flat because the physical reaction of belching was considered to be extremely rude.

Coloured glass can be very decorative and can make a visual statement within a room when the same colour is used or a mix of colours. The main glass colours are blue, red (ruby and cranberry), amethyst and amber – all made by adding metal oxide to the glass batch.

RIGHT These fine Regency decanters, circa 1825, are an excellent example of the lovely grey colour you should look for when buying antique crystal.

LEFT A magnificent carved marble French 17th-century portrait of the Emperor Augustus, carved by Jean Hardy.

BELOW A burr elm secretaire with ormolu detailing.

LEFT A collection of fine Victorian tea caddies, boxes and objects made from antique tortoiseshell. The box in the centre at the back is parquetry of various woods.

MARBLE

All marble is old; the question is when it was carved or cut. In the eighteenth century and early nineteenth century, labour was cheap so the depth and quality of carving reached a height that was rarely achieved later on. Even on a relief the clarity and depth of carving can really bring a lifelike quality to a piece. Study the back of a plaque too for clues as to age. Earlier pieces were handmade, so the backs were rougher rather than neatly cut.

Identifying marbles is time consuming as there are so many different types. Carrara, from Italy, should be pure white on fine antique pieces. Now it is almost impossible to obtain in this state, as it nearly always has grey veins. Two other types used extensively on Grand Tour pieces are Sienna and Marmo Rosso. Sienna is still available, but is not as beautiful as it used to be.

Pietra dure inlay is a term that describes using marbles and semi-precious stones to create a picture or pattern – a skilled, time-consuming and therefore expensive process. This type of work is still produced today in India and Italy. Scagliola is imitation *Pietra dure*, made of ground marble paste and colouring. Good seventeenth- and eighteenth-century scagliola table tops are much sought after.

BRONZE

Copper and tin alloy has existed for 4,000 years, but you are most likely to find it in pieces from the eighteenth and nineteenth centuries. Most have been gilded – where gold has been applied to the surface – or patinated. The latter is a way of making a piece look old. Quality is important, so study the difference in finishes so that you can appreciate the best when you find it.

Not everything made in the eighteenth century is considered better than that of the nineteenth. Ormolu, or gilt bronze, was definitely of better quality and finish in the early nineteenth century than it was a hundred years earlier. The gilt bronze mounts, handles and decoration, on a suite of furniture made by Jean-Jacques Werner (1791–1849), for example, far outstrip those on most eighteenth-century pieces. Likewise his attention to detail with his use of woods and inlays easily matches those of the eighteenth century.

Another example of fine quality bronze is the pair of Austrian engraved crystal urns on page 171: the casting and chasing is second to none. Age, rarity and provenance are all important, and prices on exceptional bronze pieces can reach some dizzy heights.

ANTIQUITIES

This term refers to items which are thousands of years old as opposed to hundreds. It includes objects from ancient civilizations – Rome, Egypt, Greece, near eastern and China. It is a very specialized area and professional advice should be sought before buying, so that you can be sure about the authenticity of what you are buying.

TORTOISESHELL

The first thing to remember is that all items made from tortoiseshell are covered by the Convention of International Treaty on Endangered Species, so the appropriate paperwork is required when a piece is shipped. This also applies to ivory and shagreen.

Tortoiseshell or turtle shell is so difficult to repair that it is not advisable to buy any that needs restoration. Even polishing these items is time consuming. Tortoiseshell tea caddies have gone up in value tremendously. However, there are also plenty of fake Georgian ones around, mainly produced in the Philippines – so beware of imitations. A favourite trick is to use a period wooden caddy and re-veneer in new tortoiseshell. Green or red ones are very rare and extremely expensive. Tortoiseshell inlaid with silver or gold was mostly made at the end of the nineteenth century. Known as piqué, it has become very expensive. Small eighteenth-century piqué boxes are quite specialist, but acquire pleasing decorative value when used in collections.

IVORY

New ivory should not be bought in the country of origination, because it is illegal to bring it home. A smooth piece of ivory is almost impossible to repair invisibly and so consequently repairs are fairly obvious. Prices vary enormously depending on the object, with intricately carved and lathe-turned pieces being hugely sought after as they make such a visual impact.

SHAGREEN

Shagreen is actually shark or ray skin. Mostly produced from 1890 to 1930, it is very collectible. Pieces of shagreen furniture are now very rare, but it is possible to find decorative objects. It comes in a variety of colours, but most commonly is green. It can be smooth or quite rough and is quite often combined with silver or gilt bronze. Once again, restoration is definitely a professional task.

ABOVE This Dutch 19th-century tortoiseshell mirror has ebonized mounts and unusually, a crest.

RIGHT A fine example of carved ivory, which dates from 19th-century Africa.

BELOW A splendid collection of lathe-turned ebony-and-ivory 19th-century candlesticks, some of which were made in India.

INDEX

AUTHORS' ACKNOWLEDGEMENTS & CREDITS

Genevieve Weaver: I would like to say thank you to all those who have worked with me over the years to make Guinevere what it is today, in particular to John Arnett who accompanied me on buying trips from almost the very beginning, and continues to do so even when he would much prefer to have his feet up at home. To my sons Kevin and Marc, and their wives Caroline and Heather, without whom none of it would now be possible. To Rob Hunter who has put up with all my moods and whose eye for detail has been a continuous inspiration. To Michael Folkard who seems to understand what I want before I have even thought about it. To all the staff, past and present, who have helped Guinevere gain the recognition it now enjoys. To all those I have bought from over the years, many of whom were generous in their support, encouragement and knowledge. And finally to all those I have sold to, because it is they who have enabled Guinevere to play its part as a design catalyst, linking styles and ideas from the past to those of the future.

Helen Chislett: Genevieve Weaver and I would like to say thank you to Theo Woodham-Smith for making the book possible in the first place, and to all those at Collins & Brown who worked so hard to bring our idea to fruition We would also like to express our gratitude to all the designers - and their clients - who allowed us into their homes to photograph antiques in context. Last - but by no means least - I would like to say thank you to my husband John who has given me unfailing support, both verbal and practical, in the writing of this book.

With grateful thanks to the following designers:
Alidad: pp 39, 43, 56, 66, 75, 134, 135, 136, 137; Nina Campbell: pp 65(top), 151, 152; Marie-Luis Charmat: pp 26/7, 28, 31, 32/3, 45, 50, 55, 74, 124; Lilli Curtiss: pp 146, 147, 148, 149; Vivien Greenock of Sybil Colefax and John Fowler: pp 125; David A Harte: pp 23, 29, 35, 41, 63, 82, 85, 88/9, 122; Rob Hunter: pp 5, 64, 65(bottom), 72, 83, 92, 93, 94, 95, 162, 163, 165(top); Chester Jones: pp 52, 53, 59, 78, 79, 90, 101; John Minshaw: pp 1, 34, 48, 49, 77, 104, 107, 112, 113, 126, 127, 128, 129,144, 145(bottom); Ann Mollo: pp 36, 46, 86, 87, 98, 99, 114, 118, 119, 120, 121; Wendy Nicholls of Sybil Colefax and John Fowler: pp 40, 111, 153; Jonathan Reed (Reed/Boyd Partnership): pp 54, 58, 91, 142, 143, 145(top); Renoir Designs: pp 38, 81, 84, 106, 110, 123, 150; Genevieve Weaver: pp 9, 30, 42, 60, 68/69, 102, 103, 105, 115, 158, 159, 160, 161; Kevin Weaver: pp 97, 100, 108, 109, 130, 131, 132, 133, 165(bottom); Marc & Heather Weaver: pp 22, 47, 68, 80, 154, 155, 156, 157; Judy Wilder: pp 25, 116/7

Photographer's credits
Copyright is owned by the photographer or the designer unless otherwise stated. Every effort has been made to trace the copyright holders. Collins & Brown apologise if any omissions have been made.
Collins & Brown/Andreas Von Einsiedel pp 1-2, 5-6, 12, 17-18, 23-24, 29-30, 34, 36-39, 41-44, 46, 49, 52, 56-57, 61-67, 70-73, 75-76, 81-89, 92-100, 102-106, 108-110, 112-115, 118-123, 126, 129-141, 146-152, 158-165, 167 (below), 168 (top and below), 169 (top and below), 170 (top and below), 171 (top and below), 172 (top and below), 173 (all)
Andreas Von Einsiedel pp 22, 47, 53-54, 58-59, 68-69, 78-80, 90-91, 101, 127-128, 142-145, 154-157
Peter Johnson pp 8-10
Henry Wilson p 13
Clark and Hart p 15
Clive Bartlett pp 16, 19, 20-21, 60, 170 (middle), 171 (middle)
Robert Brown pp 25, 116
Fritz von der Schulenberg pp 26, 50, 124
Colefax and Fowler group pp 40, 111, 125, 153
Michael Hoppen p 169 (middle)
Paul Redmond pp 34, 48, 77, 107